twenties
LONDON

twenties
LONDON
A City in the Jazz Age

Cathy Ross

MUSEUM OF LONDON

Philip Wilson Publishers

First published in 2003 by
Philip Wilson Publishers Ltd
7 Deane House
27 Greenwood Place
London NW5 1LB

Distributed in the UK by
I.B. Tauris & Co. Ltd
6 Salem Road
London W2 4BU

Distributed in the USA and Canada by
Palgrave Macmillan (St Martin's Press)
175 Fifth Avenue
New York NY 10010

ISBN 0-85667-568-7 (cloth)
0-904818-99-3 (paperback)

Written, designed and photographed by the Museum of London to accompany the exhibition, 1920s: the decade that changed London (16 October 2003 – 20 July 2004). Not all items shown in this volume appear in the exhibition.

Editor: Mark Kilfoyle
Designer: Benjamin de Lotz
Photographers: John Chase and Richard Stroud

Acknowledgements
The author would like to thank the following for their help with the research and production of this book: Emma Shepley of the Museum of London who assisted with most aspects of the content, Harry Wykes and Chris Judge Smith of the Kibbo Kift Foundation, Gaynor Wells of the London Society, Michael Cudlipp and staff at the History of Advertising Trust, Amanda Huntley and staff of the London Film Archive, Neil Johannessen of British Telecom's Connected Earth, Philip Attwood, Murray Johnstone, Don Knight, Rebecca Roberts, Sehri Saklatvala, Margaret Timmers, Rozina Visram, Gordon Wellard, Anne Jackson, Norman Turpin and Cangy Venables of Philip Wilson Publishers, plus all owners and copyright holders of works illustrated here. Many colleagues at the Museum of London have helped in various ways but particular thanks are due to Heidi Britain, Edwina Ehrman, Alex Werner, Johann Hermans, Sarah Kilroy, Lucy Pringle, Kathy Rogers, John Chase and Richard Stroud for the photography, Benjamin de Lotz for the design and Mark Kilfoyle for exemplary editing. The author would also like gratefully to acknowledge the role played by the London Library, which was the source of most of the twenties publications cited here.

Cover: London's Tramways poster: 'Theatre Land' by P. Irwin Brown of Leigh Breton Studios, 1927 (detail)

Contents

Director's foreword

The ten hectic years that followed the First World War saw Britain reassess its character and London redefine its role as the nation's capital. London, more than anywhere else in the country, encapsulated the visions, desires and beliefs, both rational and irrational, that shaped Britain's future for the rest of the twentieth century.

The Museum of London is uniquely placed to tell this fascinating story, a story which has intriguing resonances with our world today and the social concerns we face at the beginning of the twenty-first century. This book, and the exhibition it accompanies, allow the Museum to emphasise London's role as a place of cultural diversity and international debate – issues which are at the very heart of the Museum's philosophy.

The *Twenties London* exhibition inaugurates the new Linbury Gallery at the Museum of London, the gift of Lord and Lady Sainsbury of Preston Candover. This new gallery for special exhibitions gives the Museum a new physical space: it is our task to use it to discuss, explore, reflect, challenge and contemplate all that London has to offer. I am delighted to invite you to join us in that task.

Professor Jack Lohman
Director

1
Bronze plaquette, 1924
Madge Kitchener (fl. 1924–37), 7.7 x 5 cm. One of eight commemorative plaquettes issued by the Royal Mint for sale at the 1924 British Empire Exhibition

Introduction

This book accompanies an exhibition whose overall aim is twofold: to communicate the exuberance of the 1920s as it was experienced in London, and to explore the decade's impact on London as a city. In pursuing this aim, both book and exhibition provide an overview, albeit an eclectic one. Both explore ideas and values as much as events, and both take as their starting point the Museum of London's collections. This has inevitably led the project to look at aspects of London's past which historians working from documents alone might not find so significant. As is inevitable for a museum whose subject is a vast and unclassifiable city, the Museum's collections cut across the divides of traditional disciplines, and it is this multi-disciplinary scope, as much as anything else, that has thrown up the particular structure taken by both book and exhibition. The first five chapters of *Twenties London* look at some of the cultural currents circulating in London during this decade. The last three chapters look more directly at the city itself, how the streets, buildings and character of London changed alongside the ebb and flow of people and ideas.

Is there an overall theme? Two intertwined strands run through all eight chapters and both are usefully 'illustrated' by C.R.W. Nevinson's 1930 painting of Fleet Street, *Amongst the Nerves of the World* (fig. 2). The first is that twenties London was indeed a place plugged into global currents of energy and ideas. In the 1920s 'nerves' was often used as a word to describe telephone systems, but London's globalness was far more than just a matter of communications. It was the world's largest city, Europe's most Americanised city with Europe's largest metropolitan working class, a port serving the world's largest Empire, and had a population incorporating people from most of the nations of the world. As such, how could twenties London not be amongst the nerves of the world? The city's experience during the 1920s, as set out here, can be seen as underlining a more general twentieth-century experience of lives being shaped by the forces of globalisation running alongside the forces of nationhood.

The nerves of the world discussed here come from America, Russia, Britain and England. It may surprise some that Europe in general and France in particular are not included. After all, in many accounts of the decorative and fine arts immediately after the First World War, France is usually placed as the nation which led while a more timid England followed. The omission of France is in no sense intended to diminish the significance of French artists on, for example, the way modern painting was understood and presented to the London public or the way Paris continued to set the looks to which London fashion houses aspired. If anything, the omission of France is in part the particular perspective this project is bringing to bear and in part because 'the French connection' has already attracted much scholarly attention and is therefore relatively well discussed compared with other aspects of the period's visual and material culture.

This is perhaps the place to add a word of explanation about terminology. The term 'art deco' is largely absent from this book because as a stylistic description coined in the sixties, it has not really proved helpful for a historical enquiry about the twenties. The twenties shorthand for the lowbrow end of the style now known as art deco was 'jazz', which is the term preferred here. The words modern and modernity will be used in the broader ways in which they were used in the 1920s, as words to be applied as much to Woolworth's chain stores as to Wyndham Lewis'

2
Amongst the Nerves of the World, 1928–30
C.R.W. Nevinson (1889–1946), oil on canvas, 76 x 50 cm. A view of Fleet Street, then the centre of the British newspaper industry

paintings. C.R.W. Nevinson's paintings from the period after the First World War have sometimes been read as evidence of Britain's reluctance to confront the modernity of the twentieth century: the country stubbornly turning its back on the future and seeking solace, instead, in a cosy traditionalism. This view of Britain between the wars is largely an art historical one, and if this account has anything to contribute to the debate, it is in support of those who see literary and artistic modernism as an 'unstable category' when discussed in isolation from the larger cultures and experiences that surrounded it.[1] London in this account is less a reluctant modernist city than a confused one, shot with diversity and criss-crossed with nervous energy as it stared at an uncertain future.

Nevinson's painting has also been read as presenting a vision of the 'controlled energy of the future,'[2] that is, energy harnessed by hierarchy and order. How to create order from the potential for disorder was something that exercised the post-war mind in almost every sphere of life. This is the second theme of the book: London as a city constantly balancing its desire for freedom and diversity against its need for controls and discipline. This was a very real dilemma for 1920s London whose inhabitants were engaged in a never-ending debate about how the city should plug itself into the energy of the modern world in a well-ordered yet non-intrusive way. From traffic lights to birth control, what checks were acceptable in the capital of a nation where individual freedom was seen as a birthright? 'London is like the English character,' wrote Sir Lawrence Weaver in 1926 about London's architecture. 'It is the stronghold of individualism . . . we will not be regulated or regimented.'[3]

Both of these themes are, of course, matters of more than historical interest. London today, at the start of the twenty-first century, is very clearly plugged into cultural currents from around the globe, and the city continues to face the eternal urban dilemma of reconciling diversity and control. This dilemma was eloquently expressed by the American novelist John Cournos, who lived in London both before and after the First World War. Cournos ranged all over the city, but the place to which he constantly returned was Speaker's Corner at Marble Arch. This, to him, was the soul of London, the microcosm not just of the city but of civilisation as a whole. It was the place that demonstrated the diversity and fragmentation at the heart of modern life: 'there was no unity, the world was here visible in all its fragmentary nature, restless in all its fractious contradiction.'[4] Modern civilisation, far from making men more homogeneous, had created a complex many-tongued civilisation: 'a community with a million persons with a million opinions.' To Cournos, Marble Arch demonstrated both the good and bad about this new chapter in the human story. The good was tolerance, a quality that he consistently associated with London in all his books. The bad was that tolerance was the very thing preventing these restless fragments ever uniting: 'But here was the appalling thing. Tolerance, one of the finest products of civilisation, was a weapon that civilisation had seemingly created for its own destruction; for if there was no common faith and unity, and it was a thing all of warring fragments, what was it worth?' This book looks at the ways twenties Londoners tried to resolve this perennial city dilemma – how to harness the diversity and energy inherent in city life to work for and with some sense of common standards and civic good.

Chapter 1

A syncopated civilisation

The soul of old England was left behind in Trafalgar Square; the bus rolled on through one of the corridors of the new England. Up Charing Cross Road past a cinema house announcing 'The Grim Avenger: a thrilling romance of Three Continents'... past a music hall, flaunting across its front the pirouetting figure of a Russian toe-dancer on a coloured screen, while underneath, flashing for the world to see, letters of bright light proclaiming other attractions: a Cockney Comedian, a Spanish Tango Turn, a Swedish Acrobat Troupe, American Clog Dancers, an Argentine 'Stunt' Artist, Naughty Fifi the French Comic Chanteuse and Mimi her Eccentric Accompanist, and so on, and so on.

How amazingly international! mused Gombarov, and laughed to himself, as the after-thought struck him: 'And here am I, a Russo-American Jew, looking on!'

Was this chaos or unity? It was chaos, and had a unity after a fashion. It was the unity of a many-tuned medley, each tune of which maintained its entity, losing it only at the moment of embracing another tune; at best, it was the unity of ultra-modern music, shaped out of discords, beaten but not molten into a harmony.

John Cournos, 1922[1]

The novel *Babel* (1922) is set in the period immediately before the First World War, but its picture of London's chaos holding together after a fashion also applies to the post-war city. At the time *Babel* was written, its author John Cournos (like his hero, Gombarov, a Russian-American Jew) was living in London, well settled into metropolitan literary life and engaged in an unhappy affair with fellow author Dorothy L. Sayers, then working as a copywriter in an advertising agency. The city he knew in the early twenties was even more bewildering on paper than it was on the streets. It remained gigantic – the western world's largest metropolis and still growing. The 1921 census saw a new population high of 7,386,875 people living within the boundaries of Greater London. 'How soon will the population reach the ten million mark?' asked the *Daily Express* in 1926 as new underground lines brought new suburbs into existence.[2] In fact the 1931 census only reached 8,110,358 people, but this represented well over one sixth of the population of Great Britain and the addition within one decade to London's teeming streets of a population the size of Birmingham, England's second largest city. In addition to the growth of official 'Greater London', the population of Middlesex, the county into which much of London's suburban developments spilled over, grew by a third between 1921 and 1931, five times the national average. The only population decline that twenties London saw was in the inner core, the area administered by the London County Council, whose population shrank slightly from 4.4 million to

3
Le 'Cabaret', 1928
Charles Laborde
(1880–1941),
hand-coloured
etching, 27 x 23 cm
(detail). Plate 5 in
*Rues et visages de
Londres*, a folio of
etchings with text by
Pierre Mac Orlan

4.3 million as those who could moved out into the fresh air and clean houses of the new suburbs. The rise in population was mirrored by a physical spread on the ground. The twenties saw a massive expansion of London's built-up area into the surrounding countryside, a process that would leave London in 1939 double the size it had been in 1919. Whichever way you looked at it, London was growing at an ever increasing rate and the process showed no signs of slowing down.

Suburban spread and population increase were among the many aspects of 1920s London which rehearsed the debate about control or *laissez faire*. Should house builders be prevented from covering the countryside with more new houses or should they just meet the demands of a free market as they saw fit? Should population increase be controlled by the 'science' of eugenics? Many in the twenties would have disagreed with Cournos' detection of unity after a fashion in London life. On the contrary, the evidence for disunity was compelling: buildings were being erected at random, people were behaving with no regard for traditional standards, traffic was getting out of control, as was the international situation: 'we are living on volcanic ground, under the continual menace of war, in the midst of obscure political preoccupations which makes us regard the future with multitudinous anxieties. Nowhere is it exactly known what is the principle of authority that must be recognised and obeyed.'[3]

This chapter will act as a broad introduction to twenties London by looking at some of the aspects of life that both provoked and exacerbated such anxieties. Foreign visitors sometimes detected in post-war London a kind of calm continuity, which suggested to them that life in London had not been much affected by the great currents of conflict that had shaken the European continent. However, the mood of twenties London was a distinctly post-war mood, and the four factors discussed below – war, democracy, science and jazz – were key ingredients in this new zeitgeist, all raising their own questions about authority and freedom, all providing rich food for thought about the future. In the words of Thomas Burke, one of London's most sensitive commentators, the real significance of the twenties was 'that it was our welcome to the new century'.[4]

The War

We are beginning to realise that [the Great War], terrible and enormous as it was, ended nothing, began nothing and settled nothing. It killed millions of people; it wasted and impoverished the world. It smashed Russia altogether. It was at best an acute and frightful reminder that we were living foolishly and confusedly without much plan or foresight in a dangerous and unsympathetic universe.

H.G. Wells, 1922[5]

The most obvious change to life before and after the First World War was of course the war itself. Britain had entered into a state of war with Germany in 1914. Four years later it emerged militarily victorious yet devastated, socially and economically. Quite apart from the mass slaughter of young men – three quarters of a million from the United Kingdom and an additional 200,000 from the Empire, a third of whom were Indians – Britain had lost wealth, influence, stability and self-confidence on an unprecedented scale. Britain had entered the war as one of the richest nations on earth. It emerged with a £900 million war debt to America, trade disrupted and economy distorted. Industrial

4
A Tank in Action, 1925–6
Sir Frank Brangwyn (1867–1950), tempera on canvas, 366 x 376 cm. One of the rejected panels for the Palace of Westminster's mural scheme for a war memorial to commemorate the lost generation of young British aristocrats

5–6
Banners, 1926
Probably designed by
John Hargrave
(1894–1982), 189 x
103 cm. Carried by
the Kindred of the
Kibbo Kift at the
final rally of the
Peacemakers
Pilgrimage in
Hyde Park in June

event whose causes were directly attributable to the war's destabilising effects, but there were many other upheavals. In 1918 the overthrow of old regimes in Poland, the Balkans and Austria was followed by revolution in Germany which brought a shaky new republic into being. The fascist revolution in Italy in 1922 brought Mussolini onto the European stage. Within the countries that then formed part of the British Empire, calls for Home Rule took on a more impatient and angry tone. Ireland erupted into a bitter civil war, which led to the death of thousands and political assassinations on the streets of London. Any hint of nationalist unrest in India was put down with ferocity. The Aegean crisis saw Turkish troops threaten British garrisons. There was violence in the Sudan in 1924, China in 1925 and Egypt in 1926, plus the ever present backdrop of Russia, desperately struggling to consolidate its new regime in the face of terrible famine and international hostility. All suggested that the world was entering a new era, one in which political change was as likely to come quickly through violence as slowly through peaceful evolution.

Conflicts in distant lands were brought home to the Londoner through newspapers and magazines. The *Illustrated London News* assiduously reported world events with illustrations that were sometimes harrowingly graphic. To add to the gloom the magazine also drew to its readers' attention to the latest developments in scientific warfare. In 1924 alone, readers were told about a terrible new American phosphorous bomb, a death-dealing rocket which would rain down molten metal and a devastating new 'light-ray' that would destroy aircraft as if by lightning.[6] All were presented as weapons for use in the next war, a thought which no doubt led Londoners to the

relations deteriorated sharply when a frenetic and short-lived boom in the immediate post-war years turned into a catastrophic slump. Mass unemployment threw a new and sinister shadow over the nation's future as the 700,000 unemployed workers in 1920 increased to the million mark in March 1921 and two million by the end of the year. Throughout the rest of the decade unemployment ebbed and flowed between the one and two million mark, never allowing itself to be forgotten.

Quite apart from the problems directly attributable to the conflict, the war was also seen as a kind of Pandora's box from which had escaped a virulent strain of international instability. The Russian revolution of 1917 was the most shocking political awful conclusion that war was now the normal state for world affairs. Aerial warfare was a particular fear for the future. The First World War had seen London's first ever experience of aerial bombing, and the bombs had also brought the realisation that wars of the future would threaten not just soldiers at the front but also civilians at home. These fears were reflected at the British Empire Exhibition of 1924 when, as part of the government pavilion displays, the War Office showed an audio-visual presentation making the case for a national air raid defence system. In *London Defended* the audience was shown two scenarios: in the first a foreign power declares war on Britain, London is undefended from the air and consequently destroyed. In the second version, London is protected and survives.

To many, far from being the war to end all wars or 'The War for Civilisation', as the legend on Britain's war medals had it, the war of 1914–18 was a terrible premonition of a barbaric future. 'War Won't Work', 'Life or Death' were the messages on banners made for the Peacemakers Pilgrimage which took place in Hyde Park in June 1926, as the culminating point of a march from many parts of England (figs 5 and 6). The Hyde Park event was said to have been attended by 7000 supporters who passed a resolution urging that international disputes be resolved by arbitration rather than war and then performed a symbolic pageant, 'The Coming of Peace'.

The reservations that surrounded Britian's victory can also be detected in the progress of Sir Frank Brangwyn's scheme of mural decoration for the Royal Gallery in the House of Lords at the Palace of Westminster. The artist was commissioned by Lord Iveagh in 1926 to paint a scheme which would serve as a War Memorial to the Peers who had lost

their lives in the War. Brangwyn's initial scheme was made up of powerful scenes of battle (fig. 4). However, after two years work this scheme was abandoned, apparently on the joint decision of Iveagh and Brangwyn who decided themselves that the mud and blood were too strong to stomach: they were, it was reported, 'reluctant to perpetuate scenes which however softened and beautified in treatment yet inevitably tended to remind spectators of the miseries of war.'[7] Instead they settled on a scheme depicting 'the glories of Empire, which these men died to save,' a subject which enabled Brangwyn to produce something equally powerful but evocative of lushness and fertility rather than wretchedness and death.

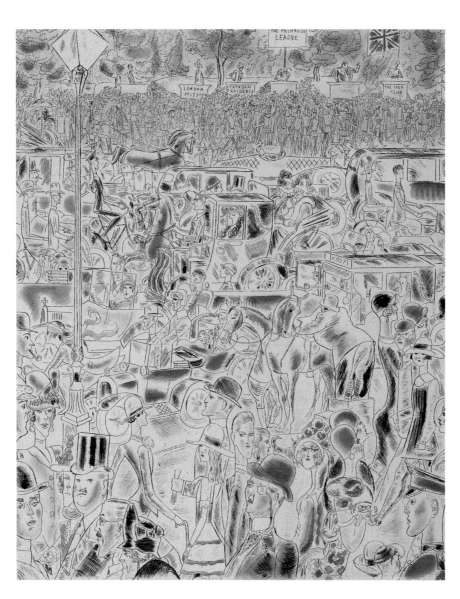

7
*Hyde Park
(Rotten Row),* 1928
Charles Laborde
(1880–1941), hand-
coloured etching,
27 x 23 cm. Plate 21
from *Rues et visages
de Londres,* a folio of
etchings with text by
Pierre Mac Orlan

Democracy

*We hear a great deal about the terrors of modern
invention, with its power of indiscriminate slaughter,
but what terrifies me far more is the modern mind.*
C.R.W. Nevinson, 1937[8]

Perhaps the most significant and far-reaching
change in British society before and after the First
World War was the arrival of mass democracy.
The first and largest of the two steps that brought
democracy to Britain was the Representation of
the People Act of 1918 which transformed the
British political system to a revolutionary degree.
The act enfranchised more people than the other
three preceding reform bills put together and

nearly tripled the electorate from 7.5 million
to over 20 million people. It not only gave
women over thirty the vote, but by enfranchising
vast tranches of the male population, including
paupers, cut the centuries-old link between voting
and property ownership. For the first time Britain
embraced the notion of an organic, inclusive state
in which all those whose lives were touched in
any way by its activities had a right to say how
the state was run. In 1918 this of course did not
yet include women between the ages of twenty-
one and thirty who had to wait until 1929,
when the second Representation of the People
Act completed the process by which the British
electoral system at long last reached theoretical
democracy. The arrival of the 'flapper vote' in that

8
A Prophecy, 1929
Batt [Oswald Charles Barrett] (1892–1945),
37 x 26 cm. A comment on the 'flapper election'
drawn for *The Railway Review*

year reactivated some of the old arguments that the irresponsible, however charming and radiant, should not be trusted with such serious matters as politics. Oswald Barrett (fig. 8) was unusual among cartoonists in offering a more optimistic view.

Historians have pointed out that the word 'democracy' did not enter into common usage until the twenties, and it was only really in that decade that Britain became aware that it was in fact a democratic state. The word was bandied about a lot in the 1920s as a kind of modern novelty, usually describing something or somewhere which appealed across social classes. Lyons Corner House restaurants were democratic, as was the British Empire Exhibition of 1924 and the new West End super-cinemas. The greyhound racing which started up at Wembley Stadium in 1927 aimed to appeal to all and be as democratic as the horse racing at Epsom. The opening night of the British National Opera Company in 1922 was praised for the diverse audience it attracted, 'largely no doubt by reason of the democratic basis on which the company is organised.'[9] Democracy was a word which often appeared on the lips of the Prince of Wales. In May 1922 at a speech at the Royal Academy, he called advertising poster hoardings 'democracy's Royal Academy of Arts'.[10] When opening London's first municipal golf course at Richmond in June 1923, he praised its commitment to 'democratic golf' declaring that this was the place 'where artisans and royalty are equally welcome.'[11]

The idea of democracy crystallised in the popular mind during the 1920s partly as a reaction to what it was plainly not. The twenties saw the violent birth of two alternative political systems as possible bases for nationhood. From the Russian revolution of 1917 emerged Bolshevism, which established

9
The Workers, 1919
C.R.W. Nevinson (1889–1946), lithograph,
52 x 32 cm. Possibly inspired by the wave
of strikes and Bolshevik scares which swept
America in 1919. Exhibited in London in
October 1919

were those of class rather than nationhood: 'workers of the world unite' was a direct challenge not just to British democracy but also to the British Empire.

Despite the anti-Bolshevik hysteria that regularly erupted into 1920s political life, neither Bolshevism nor fascism ever posed serious political threats to Britain's new-found enthusiasm for democracy. Yet their very existence did cause reflections on the character of the system of parliamentary democracy that had evolved, on the whole peacefully, over the last few centuries. Democracy was not universally welcomed. There were those who regretted that this latest franchise extension had brought with it a cultural degradation: 'political progress has outstripped civilisation.'[12] There were those who felt that democracy was the worst possible system of government for the modern world, which demanded quick thinking about complex matters. There were those who worried about the assumptions of the British system now that Freud had concluded that man was basically irrational: if individual men and women were irrational, then the masses were terrifyingly so and mass democracy had irrationality built into it. The point of view which held that human progress would be better served by the Bolshevik or fascist model of a small elite making the masses' decisions for them was not as unusual in the twenties as it was later to become.

On the other hand, there were those who welcomed the new interest taken by the masses in politics. The journalist H.G.W. Nevinson, father of the painter, considered that politics was now second only to sport in engaging the enthusiasm of the working man, a development he put down in part to the government's increasing intervention into matters of daily life, as well as the new democracy.[13] The Labour Party was also a natural champion of democracy since the 1918 act had transformed their

government by an elite group in the interests of the masses. The fascist state established in Italy by Mussolini in 1922 also confined power to a small group. Both fascism and Bolshevism were generally seen as running counter to every value Britain held dear: both systems espoused violence as a tool for political change; both diminished individual freedoms in the interests of strong state control; neither were 'democratic'. Of the two, Bolshevism was generally presented as the political system most threatening to British values for its insistence that the only divisions that really mattered in the world

10
1925 Wembley, 1925
C.R.W. Nevinson (1889–1946), lithograph, 88 x
61 cm. A design for a bus poster promoting the
second season of the British Empire Exhibition

political fortunes. From thirty-nine members of
parliament before the 1918 franchise reforms, the
party grew to 288 members of parliament in 1929,
and the twenties saw the start of their track record
in government with their first, short-lived
administration of 1924.

If the democratic masses were more visible in the
political landscape, they were also more visible on the
London streets. The transport revolution begun in the
Edwardian period had given London a mass transport
system unique in Europe. Already in place before the
First World War were London's networks of electric
trams, electric railways and electric tubes. By the
1920s the revolution gathered pace, giving London
the largest tram and tube systems in the world and a
rapidly expanding network of motorbus routes. Mass
transport enabled Londoners to live in the suburbs
but also brought them together in the crowded
centre. Mass crowds were the characteristic of London
that caught the attention of many visiting artists,
among them the printmaker Charles Laborde (fig. 7),
whose London crowds are, like those of Cournos,
distinct individuals squashed together in a small
space rather than a many-headed monstrous mass.
C.R.W. Nevinson's poster (fig. 10) can be taken as a
more symbolic representation of the democratic mass
in that he has incorporated all social classes: cloth
cap, homburg and bowler jostle for space in the
foreground while the top hat observes from the
side. If Nevinson was intending to make his crowd
deliberately signal democracy, he has, character-
istically, inserted a more ambiguous note into the
background, where something strange is happening –
a man holds up a megaphone and what appears to
be an explosive event has just taken place. Nevinson,
like his father, approved of the English parliamentary
tradition, but was rather more uneasy about the
wisdom of mass democracy.

11
Captain Richards' robot, 1928
This radio-controlled robot was made in
Dorking by Captain W.H. Richards and
A.H. Reffell. Its first engagement was to
open the model engineering exhibition at
the Royal Horticultural Halls.

Science

If the dangers, confusions and disasters that crowd upon man in these days are enormous beyond any experience of the past, it is because science has brought him such powers as he never had before. And the scientific method of fearless thought, exhaustively lucid statement and exhaustively criticised planning, which has given him these as yet uncontrollable powers, gives him also the hope of controlling these powers.

H.G. Wells, 1922[14]

By the 1920s science's power to work miracles in the material world was a well-established fact of life. Readers of the *Illustrated London News* were brought a succession of ever more astonishing inventions, all explained by diagrams: transatlantic automatic telephones, electronic transmission of pictures, colour cinematography, air traffic control systems, talking pictures. These technological miracles were remarkable in themselves but in one sense not unusual: they conformed to what the public had come to expect from science, which had been pulling off trick after astonishing trick since the nineteenth century. However, the 1920s bought two new aspects to the popular understanding of science and how it was shaping human life.

The first was automation, the arrival of machines which not only helped mankind work more efficiently but which eliminated the human element entirely. The main examples in twenties London were automatic telephone exchanges, automatic ticket dispensers, automated production in factories, and the Totalisator or automatic bookie. 'A one-man job – a symbol of our time', said the *Illustrated London News* in 1929, printing a dramatic photograph by E.O. Hoppé of a single

man at the switchboard of a vast power station in Berlin whose machinery otherwise ran itself.[15] The other symbol of our time was the the robot, or machine-made replacement for man (fig. 11). The term robot had been popularised in London by Karel Capek's play, *Rossum's Universal Robots*, seen on the London stage in 1923. Thereafter robots appeared all over the place, opening exhibitions, marching in pageants and dancing at fancy dress balls. Most famously, a robot took a starring role in Fritz Lang's allegorical film *Metropolis*, which was premiered in London in March 1927 (fig. 12), and which prophesied terrible things to come should automatic machinery end up enslaving mankind.

Despite the *Metropolis* prediction, automation effectively sidestepped many of the old complaints about machines as tyrannical enslavers of humans. Automatic machinery had the potential to be an agent of liberation, freeing men and women from toil and ushering in new opportunities for self-development. Radical thinkers predicted that automatic machinery would bring the end of work and the dawning of a new age of leisure. But this too brought dilemmas. Leisure in theory was unemployment in practice and the twenties had ample evidence of the human misery that unemployment could bring, particularly in the north of England. Even in London, the future welfare of telephone operators made redundant by the automatic exchanges became a cause for concern. Less tears were shed about the bookies, particularly as London's first totalisator was installed as a novelty in a London gaming club.[16] When in 1929 the tote moved to the masses at Harringay's newly erected 'democratic' greyhound stadium, it raised new questions. Was the tote a morally good thing for being a cleaner, scientific

12
**Metropolis
programme, 1927**
25 x 19 cm.
The cover of the
programme for the
British premiere of
Fritz Lang's film
held at the Pavilion
Cinema, Marble Arch
on 21 March 1927

and controlled way of betting, or was it morally bad for making betting too easy?

The second new aspect of science in the 1920s, and one that was equally impossible to place as morally good or bad, was the new science of psychology. It was constantly pointed out, usually by old scientists, that psychology was technically not a science at all in that it was an imprecise art and had no scientific laws with which to make accurate predictions. Nevertheless, it did seem to offer new ways of understanding the world and many people believed that as the new science developed, so its laws would emerge which would one day give mankind the power to predict precisely every nuance of human behaviour, thus making all policing, crime, politics and romance redundant.

Unlike Einstein's theories, which crept into the public domain at about the same time, people took to Freud's theories enthusiastically. Most people were fascinated by the notion that inside them was a vast, hitherto undiscovered, dark sea called the subconscious and that it was this subconscious that determined what they did, rather than their rational conscious mind. The sensation of 1922 in London was the French psychologist Emile Coué who preached 'the healing power of the imagination exercised by the unconscious self.'[17] According to Coué, the unconscious self was the undisputed master of human behaviour and always stronger than the will. The prescription for self-improvement was therefore a simple matter of giving the unconscious self a daily dose of positive thinking by chanting 'every day in every way I am getting better and better.'

A rudimentary awareness of psychology permeated virtually every aspect of both public and private life in twenties London. In public life, as we shall see, it changed the way products were sold, politics were discussed and governments presented themselves. In private it was one of the factors in the general relaxing of codes of behaviour that the twenties saw. The notion that repressing emotions was a cause of mental illness and that good mental health was cultivated by deliberately not bottling up emotions or suppressing desires was welcomed, perhaps particularly by women. The new science, whatever its imprecisions, did have a lasting effect on British society in helping both men and women shed some of the burden of sin and shame associated with certain aspects of traditional British behaviour.

If the one-man worker and the robot were two symbols of the twenties, a third was the twenties version of 'The New Woman'. The New Woman clearly existed in that she walked about the streets of London and was the subject of endless discussion in newspapers and magazines. She was recognisable by her short shingled hair, supposedly mannish manner and association with all things modern. But where had she come from? Was she a creature of political emancipation? Was she a product of biological evolution – one theory was that these creatures represented an entirely new 'third sex'.[18] Was she in some way a product of cold science, like the robot in *Metropolis* who conspicuously lacked all the traditional feminine qualities of love and compassion that her human counterpart so gushingly displayed?

The New Woman of the twenties was, of course, a mixture of many things. Hard science had certainly played a role: from the technology of office work, which had opened up new opportunities for women's employment, to the technology of birth control, which began to be openly discussed in the 1920s thanks to the crusading zeal of Marie Stopes. Science, it was

13
Everyday Life in 2030, 1930
E. McKnight Kauffer (1891–1954), 15.5 x 10.5 cm.
One of nine bookplates in *The World in 2030*AD by
the Earl of Birkenhead

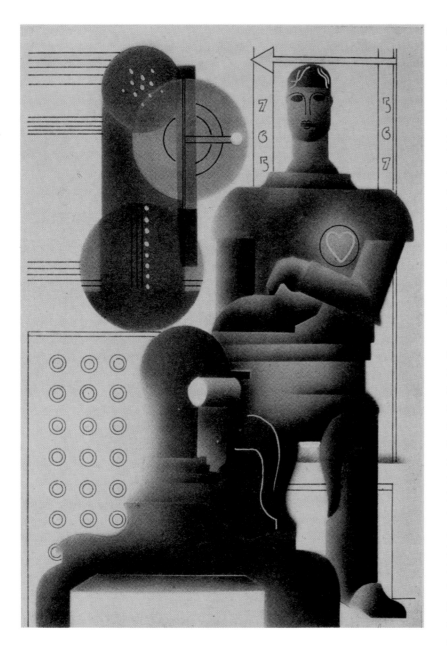

assumed, would also play a key role in the future of not just the middle-class New Woman, but also women in general. Several scientists, taking the trends of the twenties to their logical conclusions, predicted that in the not too distant future women would divorce themselves completely from the messy and dangerous business of childbirth, giving birth instead by 'ectogenesis', that is outside the womb and in laboratories. One of the speculators on this front, Lord Birkenhead, saw this happening within the next hundred years and that this, 'the most serious biological departure since the natural separation of living organisms into two sexes, will vitally transform the whole status of women in society.'[19] He himself approved, seeing the new process of childbirth as prevailing over the old because of its 'advantages of efficiency and logic.'

Birkenhead's vision of the future is contained in a book he published in 1930, predicting *The World in 2030*AD (fig. 13). His picture of the twenty-first century is fascinating yet, to twenty-first-century eyes, naive in its blind faith that mankind will always choose the most logical, rational and efficient solution to any problem. Birkenhead's future is a clean and quiet place where all machines are silent, people eat synthetic foods, live communally in well-ordered harmony and, when not working their sixteen-hour week, fly off to enjoy their hygienic leisure in the vast new European pleasure resort which has been created in North Africa by irrigating the Sahara desert. Most things in life will have been simplified, including men's dress which now consisted of only three outfits, one for work, one for formal occasions and one for recreation. Needless to say there is no war and every nation lives in harmony with each other because the nature of international trade means war is in no one's interest.

14
Jazz canister, 1930
13 x 9 cm. A bookplate from *Pitman's Dictionary of Advertising and Printing* using a 'jazz canister' to demonstrate the use of British Standard trichromatic inks

Birkenhead's is a patrician vision of the future, almost eighteenth century in its optimism that heavy doses of rationality and logic will improve the human condition. At the same time he was absolutely characteristic of one sort of 1920s mind, one which believed with a fervour bordering on zealotry that science held the key to the future, not just in the technological advances it brought, but also in the attitudes of mind associated with the scientific method: rational planning, logical decision-making and a preference for order.

Jazz

Jazz is the product of a restless age; an age in which the fever of war is only now beginning to abate its fury; when men and women, after their efforts in the great struggle, are still too much disturbed to be content with a tranquil existence . . . when America is turning out her merchandise at an unprecedented speed and motor cars are racing along the roads . . . when the extremes of Bolshevism and Fascismo are pursuing their own ways simultaneously and the whole world is rushing helter skelter in unknown directions.
R.W.S. Mendl, 1927[20]

The opposite of the clinical, ordered harmony that science promised for the future was the unpredictable, fragmented excitement that people in the 1920s associated with the word 'jazz'. Jazz was, of course, primarily a type of music, but the word in the twenties was also an all-purpose adjective which could be applied to almost anything, from clashing colours and loud patterns to anti-social behaviour and traffic noise. On the London stage, *The Jazz Marriage* (1925) played out a modern tale of divorce. In the London shops there were jazz consumer goods (fig. 14) and jazz clothes. To jazz was to dance frenziedly but 'jazzing up' or 'jazzing', as in 'jazzing the classics', was to make a new, irreverent version of a usually more sedate original, disregarding all the accepted conventions of form, harmony and taste. Jazz was associated with unharnessed energy, revolt against convention and youth.

Patricians like Lord Birkenhead were violently opposed to jazz in all its forms. So too were many others. Anna Pavlova found jazz dancing 'disgusting',[21] Aldous Huxley railed against 'the rhythmic throbbing . . . wailing glissandos . . . appalling lack of subtlety' of the music.[22] The Design and Industry Association condemned the tendency of modern graphic design to head in the direction of 'negroid chaos and jazz'.[23] Most notoriously, Clive Bell, in his petulant essay 'Plus de Jazz', dismissed not just the music but also James Joyce, whose literary technique of fragmented narrative he accusingly identified as jazz, 'that school whose grand object is to present, as surprisingly as possible, the chaos of any mind at any given moment. The Jazz theory of art, if theory there be, seems stupid enough.'[24] Bell stood fair and square for standards and order, a hard-line enforcer of the divide that began to open up in the 1920s between highbrows and lowbrows, terms that passed into popular understanding in that decade. 'Brows are being worn low this season,' said a reviewer of the Everyman Theatre in 1927. 'No more Nordic Gloom, Italian Expressionism nor Spanish Poesy. Instead noisy gaiety, blaring Jazz and barking dogs.'[25]

Jazz the music was, of course, firmly in the lowbrow camp – not only for its perceived failure to conform to any highbrow aesthetic standards, but also for its association with mass culture, and in particular with the commercial exploitation of mass culture. 'The highbrows disdain jazz music,' wrote the *Musical Standard* in 1927, 'but no-one can deny that there is money in it.'[26] Fortunes were certainly made in the growing recorded music industry and the entertainment circuit of night clubs and dance halls for the music perfectly caught the mood of post-war London: it was modern, irresistibly danceable and glamorously American.

Jazz as live music arrived in London in 1919 in the shape of the Original Dixieland Jazz Band, a group of white Italian-American musicians from Chicago who took up residency at the Hippodrome, the London Palladium and finally the Hammersmith Palais de Danse, a vast new American-style luxury dance hall which became something of a mecca for suburban West London in the 1920s. The Hammersmith Palais was very lowbrow – massive, glamorous and unashamedly commercial with its system of professional partners. Interestingly, contemporary accounts describe a far more well-ordered experience than jazz's reputation for chaotic abandon would suggest. At Hammersmith, 'orthodox evening attire' was compulsory and codes of behaviour on the dance floor stricter than the West End: 'No Haymarket antics permitted at Hammersmith.'[27] Malcolm Drummond's view (fig. 15) certainly conveys a sense of order. The separate couples move in their own self-absorbed orbits, the oriental decoration and Japanese composition creating a rather un-jazz-like sense of balance and harmony. This is a very English floating world of transient and slightly melancholic pleasure. William Roberts (fig. 16) gives a more discordant and perhaps more highbrow impression of jazz. Here the dancing is an equally engrossing but considerably less lyrical experience. This painting was exhibited at the Chenil Galleries in 1923 where its angular style was seen as perfectly matched to its urban subject matter: 'Mr Roberts has first of all an intimate knowledge of

15
Hammersmith Palais de Danse, 1920
Malcolm Drummond (1880–1945), oil on canvas, 71 x 51 cm

16
The Jazz Party, 1921
William Roberts (1895–1980),
oil on canvas, 76 x 106 cm

the more characteristic aspects of contemporary urban life and he has worked out a convention which enables him to present them in a forcible manner with an insistence on the grotesque which is calculated to make them stick in the mind.'[28]

The highbrow/lowbrow divide did not necessarily run along class lines. Jazz music and jazz behaviour were taken up enthusiastically by London's upper classes, including the Prince of Wales. Where jazz did bring out more traditional divisions in British society was the matter of race. As a music, jazz represented the culture not just of an alien nation, America, but also of races that were considered at the time not to have moved so far from their 'primitive' state as Europeans had. The association with 'Negro culture' was reinforced in London by the black American musicians who were bought across the Atlantic *en masse* after the war to replace the Germans who had staffed London's popular orchestras before.[29] Among the new arrivals in 1919 was Will Cook's Southern Syncopated Orchestra, offering a more refined musical experience than its competitors, but uniformly black and containing in its front line the young but already remarkable clarinet virtuoso Sidney Bechet.

Jazz's alien associations were further underlined by the link often made in the 1920s between jazz and Jewishness, due largely to the fact that popular music's finest composers, men such as George Gershwin, Irving Berlin and Cole Porter, were indeed Jewish. Twenties London did not escape the anti-semitic asides that complaints about jazz often expressed, alongside the racist assumptions about black culture that usually formed the core of the complaint. In London there was a visibly strong Jewish link, thanks to the vigorous musical culture of the Jewish East End, which supplied many of the musicians, singers, publishers and entrepreneurs

who made up London's popular music industry. London's largest record shop was Levy's of White-chapel, which also made its own recordings and has been claimed as Britain's first record label.

Despite its cosmopolitan associations, jazz was also thought to represent the primitive. To English ears in the 1920s the reference point for strange brassy sounds, complex drum rhythms and passages of improvisation performed by black musicians was not urban America but tribal Africa. Although by strange coincidence the music perfectly matched the mood of the twentieth-century noisy urban world, the common assumption was that jazz had nothing at all to do with the evolution of Western civilisation but came directly from the jungle. This had the perhaps unfortunate effect of linking jazz in some vague way with the British Empire, a point that was illustrated in 1926 when a painting by John Souter entitled *The Breakdown*, an allegory on Western civilisation which paired a black Negro saxophonist with a naked white woman, was removed from the Royal Academy on the complaint of the Colonial Office who had been persuaded that the image had subversive potential.[30] Although never seen as a political threat in the way that Bolshevism was, jazz was certainly seen by some sections of the Establishment with vague unease as an alien energy that threatened to capture the souls of the British working class, leaving them devitalised, deracinated and regressing to a savagely unmanageable state of robotic frenzy.

All in all, jazz as music and as a wider cultural style posed something of a puzzle for 1920s London. What sort of future was it pointing to: one of fragmented chaos or exhilarating possibilities? Was it a sign of modern vigour or modern breakdown? Was Britain's cultural future one of highbrow standards or lowbrow mass enthusiasms? Perhaps it is no coincidence that the firmest opinion on the matter

17
**Sidney Bechet,
1922**
The musician Sidney
Bechet (1898–1991)
photographed by the
Metropolitan Police
on his arrest in
September 1922

came from a European. Eugene Ansermet, the composer and conductor, was one of several highbrow Europeans, among them Darius Milhaud, who took the opportunity provided by London to see real American jazz played live. In 1920 Ansermet was in London as musical director of Diaghilev's *Ballets russes* and attended a concert given at the Queen's Hall by Will Cook's Southern Syncopated Orchestra. In a rhapsodic review Ansermet singled out the 'extraordinary clarinet virtuoso' whose improvisations were 'extremely difficult [and] equally admirable for their richness of invention, force of accent and daring in novelty and the unexpected . . . Their form was gripping, abrupt, harsh with a brusque and pitiless ending like that of Bach's second Brandenburg concerto. I wish to set down the name of this artist of genius; as for myself I shall never forget it, it is Sidney Bechet.'[31] Ansermet concluded his review by wondering to himself whether this was the sound of the future, whether Bechet's music 'is perhaps the highway that the whole world will swing along tomorrow.'

Soon afterwards Bechet was deported from Britain on charges of attempted rape, charges he consistently denied (fig. 17). He returned to America with a soprano saxophone bought from an instrument shop in Soho. Soprano saxophones were uncommon at that time, and Bechet, until that point only a clarinettist, was curious as to the sound. His curiosity bore rich results, and Bechet went on to become a virtuoso on the saxophone as well as his original instrument. Sidney Bechet is, in many ways, one of the most symbolically charged people in twenties London. He embodies what John Cournos called the cultural billiard table of the Atlantic, with ideas and people propelled from America to ricochet between London and Paris before being shot back again.[32] Bechet is also a reminder that the future that was being shaped in 1920s London was not just one of rational order, standards and control but also a more unpredictable and vital one of improvisation, individual expression and cultural syncopation.

Chapter 2

America

*When I am rich, I shall ask Thomas Derrick, who is easily the funniest cartoonist in England . . .
to draw me a cartoon, all for myself and my friends, showing Lord Beaverbrook and Messrs.
Blumenfeld and Selfridge in a little room, poring over a map of England and dividing it up among
themselves, like those chaps in 'Julius Caesar'. Because that is what is happening; and who cares?*

Glyn Roberts, 1933[1]

By the early 1930s the metaphor of conquest to describe the American presence in England was something of a cliché. In 1903, Max Beerbohm had produced a cartoon portrait of C.T. Yerkes, the American underground railway magnate, entitled 'One of our conquerors'. In 1926 the *Illustrated London News* drew its readers' attention to 'a new force in the American invasion', which was 'the steerage scholar', college students coming to Europe to broaden their education.[2] The cartoon that accompanied the report depicted this new wave of invaders as loudly dressed 'rubber necks', but however superior the British might feel, few doubted that, for better or worse, America was rapidly eclipsing Britain as the world's top nation.

Beaverbrook, Blumenfeld and Selfridge were all from the world of business: respectively the Canadian-born owner of the *Daily Express*, his American editor-in-chief and the Chicago-born founder of the mammoth department store in Oxford Street (which had opened in 1909 but grew to its eleven-acre final size in the 1920s, making it the biggest commercial premises in Europe). The activities of these plutocrats were just one aspect of the Americanisation of life in London during the 1920s. There were many others. Looking back from the 1930s, Thomas

Burke began to list the many American-inspired changes that London had seen since the turn of the century:

Our tube railways we owe to America. The bulk of our entertainment is American in quality and largely in personnel. All our latest hotels derive from American models. Our snack-bars and all-night supper-stands are pirated from America. Our electric night-signs are an American idea. Our street songs are American. Our popular press models itself on American journalism, and on our book stalls English periodicals lie smothered and half-seen under piles of American magazines.

He went on to mention American-style buildings, one-way streets and automatic traffic controls, American-style giant stores and roadhouses. Finally 'the new verve of our social occasions and the mixing of all classes are American traits.' This first section of the twentieth century, predicted Burke, would go down in history as 'London's American Phase'.[3]

This chapter will look at just three aspects of this multi-fronted Americanisation. Firstly, the new social verve of London's rich and privileged as the British

18
Bush House by Night, 1927
William Larkins (1901–74), etching, 26 x
33 cm. The view shows the building before
the erection of the two side wings. In 1932
Larkins was to find employment in Bush
House as art director for the advertising
agency J. Walter Thompson.

upper class reconstituted themselves along more glamorous American lines. Secondly, the reorganisation of English retailers and manufacturers in imitation of American models of mass production and mass selling. The final section of this chapter is devoted to advertising: 'one of the mightiest and consequently one of the most dangerous forces in the modern world.'[4] Advertising was neither an American invention nor a 1920s phenomenon, but it was during the 1920s that the British advertising industry swelled in scope, self-consciousness and scientific application, very much in emulation of trends across the Atlantic.

It must be stressed that twenties London genuinely welcomed the American invasion, although a groundswell of anti-American rumblings was kept up by traditionalists throughout the decade. For most, this was a brotherly collaboration, a coming together in friendship of two nations from the same family tree: America was the dynamic younger brother, whose energy and ideas complemented the wisdom and experience of its elder sibling. The relationship was symbolically embodied by *The Friendship of the English-Speaking People*, an imposing sculptural group by Malvina Hoffman unveiled in July 1925 by the Earl of Balfour on Bush House, one of the capital's most 'American' buildings (fig. 18). Architecturally 'an attempt on the part of American architects to import their strongly nationalised ideas into the midst of London,'[5] Bush House was named after its promoter. Irving T. Bush intended his development to be a British version of his Bush House in New York, a showcase for modern manufacturers, halfway between a department store and a trade fair. For the London version, Bush imported the American architectural firm of Helmle and Corbett whose ornate stage-set of a building brought a flourish of Manhattan self-confidence to the end of Kingsway.

Society

The twenties were the great era of parties . . .
I once attended a very grand party, given by the elegant, perfumed Lord Allington and his mother. Her guests were all out of Debrett, while young Allington's friends were from the studio and the theatre. These two factions were drawn up on different sides of the room, when at a lull in the proceedings, Tallulah Bankhead, the gorgeous red-headed film star, suddenly got up and moved across the room to where Lady Cunard was sitting. Grabbing hold of Lady Cunard's dress, a skimpy affair held up on the shoulders by two tiny straps, she ripped it down to the waist, remarking in a loud gin-voice as she did so: 'I always wanted to see your tits.'

John Skeaping, 1977[6]

The incident John Skeaping recounts sums up the ingredients that made London Society after the First World War very different to London Society before. There were two distinct sets at the Allingtons' party: on the one hand, the old British aristocracy, and on the other, a rather more louche bunch. The main protagonists are both Americans. Lady Cunard was born Maud Bryce in San Francisco, but by the twenties had changed her country of residence, status and last name by marrying (and then separating from) Sir Bache Cunard, a Northampton-shire squire. By the twenties she was also in the process of changing her first name from Maud to the rather more glittering 'Emerald'. The actress Tallulah Bankhead was Alabama-born and had been brought to the London stage in 1923 by the American theatrical entrepreneur Charles B. Cochran. Bankhead's outrageous behaviour was, of course, the most obvious 'new' ingredient in British High

19
Lady Hazel Lavery, 1922
Sir John Lavery (1856–1941), oil on canvas,
127 x 102 cm. Commissioned by Emerald
Cunard, the portrait was offered to the Tate
Gallery which refused it. Lady Cunard presented
it to the Guildhall Art Gallery in 1923.

Society, creating an incident that would have been unimaginable in the sedate atmosphere of London's aristocratic drawing rooms before 1914.

The change in character and practices of London Society in this period has been well analysed by the historian Ross McKibbin. To McKibbin, the 'exclusively aristocratic and august behaviour' of Society before the First World War was replaced afterwards by a kind of 'New York Café Society'. This new Society was no less an elite than its predecessor, but based itself on glamour, fashion and wit rather than title, land and duty. It was also, in theory, more of a free market: 'above all [Society] encouraged the notion that it was in some sense "open" and therefore appropriate to a democratic age. That is why so many of its most successful members, either as party-givers or party-goers, were wealthy Americans and its essential parasites gossip-columnists . . . and film stars.'[7]

This Americanisation was most visible in the startlingly altered behaviour of the younger generation of Britain's rich and privileged, the 'Bright Young Things' who defined the hedonistic side of the decade with their non-stop partying, loud behaviour, glittering clothes and wild abandon. However, Americanisation was not just a phenomenon of youth. The British upper class had been absorbing American wealth and beauty for several generations, and by the 1920s many Americans had risen to the first rank of the British Establishment. Alongside Selfridge and Beaverbrook was Nancy Astor, the wife of the 2nd Viscount Astor who took over her husband's parliamentary seat in 1919 when he was elevated to the House of Lords and thus became Britain's first female MP. There was Grace Elvina, the American-born Lady Curzon and wife of the foreign secretary, and Lady Lavery, born Hazel Trudeau, the daughter of a

20
Lady Diana
Cooper, 1916
Ambrose McEvoy
(1878–1927), oil on
canvas, 84 x 99 cm.
McEvoy and Cooper
had studied art
together at the
Slade. This portrait,
one of many he
made of her, was
known in Diana
Cooper's family as
'The Call to Orgy'.

Chicago industrialist who had married the society portrait painter, Sir John Lavery, in 1909 (fig. 19).

One of the things the Americans brought to the British aristocracy was a lack of inhibition about their right and proper sphere of activity. Hazel Lavery, like Nancy Astor, saw female status as no bar to an active involvement in political affairs: in Hazel Lavery's case, in support of Irish Home Rule. The generation of *jeunesse dorée* that followed added a new note of positive rebellion against what were perceived as the stuffy conventions of their parents. Edith Sitwell, the daughter of Sir George Sitwell, took her rebellious mood into the worlds of avant-garde poetry and art. Diana Cooper (fig. 20), the youngest daughter of the Duke of Rutland, pursued a less angry but equally unconventional career in the more lowbrow mediums of stage and screen. A great beauty and wit, she became a fashion icon, pin-up and stage star,

uninhibited about lending her name and face to advertising campaigns. Lady Cunard's daughter Nancy also turned to avant-garde art, but combined this with a notorious hedonism and serious commitment to politically left-wing causes. Moving to Paris, she scandalised her mother by living with her black lover, the jazz musician Henry Crowder, and followed this up by publishing a remarkable, for the time, anthology of writing about black culture. *Negro* included Nancy's own rallying cry 'up with an all-Communist Harlem in an all-Communist United States!', a view that to some would have been the ultimate in shocking behaviour.[8]

London Society thus came to embrace not just old privilege but new glamour. It welcomed transatlantic stars brought to the London stage — Fred and Dorothy Astaire, Elsa Lanchester, Paul Robeson and Sophie Tucker among them. Artists, actors and

21–2
Evening shoes, 1926–9
Leather and diamanté. Made by Pluchino of
Bond Street, the shoes are from the wardrobe
of the self-styled Countess Hamon, wife of
the palm reader Cheiro.

musicians moved into the celebrity orbit, as did
showmen such as Cheiro, the Mayfair-based palm
reader whose activities led to the birth of newspaper
horoscopes in the *Sunday Express* in August 1930
(figs 21–2). The exotic Scottish theatre designer
Doris Zinkeisen (fig. 23) typified the new face of
London High Society, straddling old and new worlds
with ease through being at the same time the wife of
a naval captain, a fashionable portrait painter (whose
works hung regularly in Royal Academy summer
shows) and one of the new generation of theatre
designers whose sets and costumes breathed modern
glamour onto the London stage. Zinkeisen went on
to design for Hollywood in the 1930s, most famously
for the 1936 film of *Showboat*.

Something of the atmosphere of this new
fashionable mix, at least at its arty end, emerges
from the visitors book of the Tour Eiffel restaurant
(fig. 24). A famous avant-garde haunt before the
war, the Tour Eiffel acquired a more fashionable
edge afterwards. Alongside the English painters –
Augustus John, Nina Hamnett, Wyndham Lewis,
and C.R.W. Nevinson among them – the book
records visitors from Paris, including Jean Cocteau,
Constantin Brancusi and Tristan Tzara, perhaps
brought by Nancy Cunard who dined there with
George Moore and Aldous Huxley in 1923. The
film star Ronald Firbank visited in 1921, Charlie
Chaplin in 1922 and George Gershwin, who
inscribed in the book a little stave of music from
Rhapsody in Blue. Henry Wood also left a musical
extract alongside the note: 'I never leave
autographs.' There are visiting Americans and
English politicians. Michael Collins signed himself
'IRA chief', and in July 1930 the French painter
Raoul Dufy scribbled a picture of the Eiffel Tower
in Paris, an incident witnessed by the young
painter Nina Hamnett:

23
**Mrs Graham
Johnstone, 1929**
Doris Zinkeisen
(1898–1991), oil on
canvas, 108 x 87 cm.
Self-portrait exhibited
at the Royal Academy
in May 1929 under
the title of Zinkeisen's
married name

24
Tour Eiffel visitors book, 1921–37
Dufy's drawing for the Tour Eiffel restaurant is dedicated to its chef and patron Rudolph Stulik. Other signatures on the page include the writer Aldous Huxley and the painter Edward Wadsworth.

I heard that Raoul Dufy was in London. Being a great admirer of him I was most anxious to meet him. Lady Dean Paul was staying at the Eiffel Tower and I went there one evening in the hopes of finding her. Sitting alone in the corner was the great man. I knew him at once, although I had never seen him or even a photograph of him. He was drawing in Mr Stulik's autograph album. He was doing a drawing with a fountain pen of the Eiffel Tower in Paris. It was like a map and all the surrounding streets and buildings were all indicated correctly. He was very good looking with silvery hair and a grey suit and grey tie.[9]

The Tour Eiffel was not typical of London's fashionable night life since it had neither dance floor nor cabaret. The lifting of wartime restrictions through the replacement of the Defence of the Realm Act with the Licensing Act of 1921 led to what was described at the time as a night-club frenzy.

Hundreds of clubs were opened in the West End, from the luxurious Ciro's with its glass dance floor, the massive Kit-Cat club in the Haymarket – 'the very Stadium of Night Clubs' – to more bohemian affairs such as the Cave of Harmony, opened in Gower Street by Elsa Lanchester, or the 55 Club in Soho. Dancing was the focus of activity and dance floors were notoriously crowded, alarmingly so after the arrival of the energetic, high-kicking Charleston in 1925.

A more genuinely democratic institution than the night club was the Charity Ball. Devised by what was usually an upper-class committee, balls were designed for mass attendance and held in large venues such as the Albert Hall. Social mixing was part of the appeal: 'royalty hobnobbed with the stage; celebrities allowed themselves to be looked at; leaders of Society ogled and were ogled by professional dancers; Suburbia rubbed elbows with Mayfair and essayed nonchalance while the public eye scrutinised and the public tongue dissected them indiscriminately.'[10] Themes and fancy dress (fig. 25) were also part of the fun, as was

some form of entertaining pageant or parade. In 1928 the 'Dream of Fair Women Ball' in aid of the Winter Distress League presented a costume parade, organised by Miss Loelia Ponsonby on the theme of fashions of the past, present and future (fig. 27). The types of dress paraded to represent the women of the future were, according to *The Times*, 'a huntswoman, a bathing lady, the bridge lady, a bride's going away dress AD1950, at Ascot, a nun and a debutante in 2028.'[11]

The final element in the transformation of old money into new celebrity was the press. Britain's first gossip column appeared in the *Sunday Express* in 1926. Written by Lord Castelrosse under the persona of 'the Londoner', its perspective was that of the insider sharing intimate secrets. The appetite for such details was, according to one observer, immense:

> The interest which the whole nation takes in Society is astonishing. In continental countries for all their *snobisme* and reverence for the nobility, the masses know very little about the best people, who remain private individuals; in England people in Society are public characters. Every newspaper tells you about their private lives, every illustrated paper is perpetually publishing photographs of them and they are as much popular figures as cinema-actors are.[12]

At the same time new magazines such as *The Theatre World* (fig. 26), produced in London by an enthusiastic American Sheridan Bickers, were feeding the popular appetite for celebrity gossip from the other direction. *The Theatre World* promised a new kind of theatre publication, neither boring listings nor highbrow analysis but something with human interest about London's favourite players, 'without – of course – prying into their private lives.'[13]

25
Fancy Frocks of the Moment, c.1926
From a fancy dress catalogue produced by Weldon's of Southampton Street

26
The Theatre World, 1925
Issues 1, 2, 5 & 6, February–July. Cover designs by 'Bovey'

27
The Wedding Dress, 1928
Norman Hartnell (1901–79), silk and lace. After its starring role at the Dream of Fair Women Ball, the dress was donated to the London Museum to be 'exhibited after 1960 as a perfect specimen of our quaint period'.

Capitalism

We have become Americanised without knowing it . . . the magic combinations of mechanical science, which seem almost supernatural, mass production in manufacture and the collective forms of production, distribution and consumption triumph over the old variety of European life and level it to an increasing uniformity.

G. Ferrero, 1926[14]

If America brought zest to the upper classes, it was also seen as bringing uniformity to the middle and lower classes. To Thomas Burke: 'today we must be homogeneous or perish.'[15] He saw the craze for standardisation everywhere, and he was not alone. The evidence most frequently cited was the ubiquity of American slang, the mass-produced goods sold in chain stores, cinema – 'the esperanto of the eye', recorded music – 'the esperanto of the ear', and the suburbs. 'At first it seems that each house is different; then you realise that there are only four types tactfully arranged like chocolates in a box to give an air of variety. Each house contains the same lounge hall, the same Jacobean dining-room suite, the same (to all appearances) dear little wife.'[16]

As far as the working classes were concerned, hand-wringing about the monotony of the workers' lives went back to Victorian days. Then the monotony was usually blamed on poverty, and its devitalising effect on the people's morals. In the twenties the blame shifted to the availability of cheap goods and their devitalising effects on the people's morals. In 1925 Constance Harris went to Bethnal Green to study leisure and was dismayed to find the working classes in a state of torpor: 'the majority of them are satisfied with plenty to eat and drink, many and cheap clothes the same as everybody else buys and as little work for as much money as possible.' She was particularly dismayed by the evidence of slackness amidst plenty provided by the litter in the street: 'broken bread, orange peel, peanut shells, banana skins, half-eaten apples, fried fish and chips, bits of rag, heels off shoes, waste paper of every description.'[17]

That America was in some way implicated in this sorry state was obvious to many. America was after all the home of things done on a mass scale: massive stadiums in which thousands were entertained, massive department stores, massive buildings, mass production by machines. 'Personally I have a profound distrust of things that are done on a large scale,' wrote G.K. Chesterton in an outburst against American-style mass journalism.[18] Some would have instinctively agreed, but to many British businessmen America's superiority in the mass market pointed the way forward. The superiority of transatlantic manufacturing, production and distribution was, after all, indisputable. By 1913 the United States was producing 485,000 cars a year at an average cost of £190. Britain, by contrast, was producing 25,000 cars a year at an average cost of £325.

Two of the English firms who learned lessons from America in the 1920s were Marks & Spencer and Jo Lyons. Both were already targeting mass, rather than exclusive, markets. Marks & Spencer had begun in the 1880s as a market stall in Leeds and by 1914 had brought its Northern-style 'Penny Bazaars' to many areas of Britain, including London. Lyons, founded in 1887, had established itself with great success as a large-scale caterer, restaurant owner and food producer (fig. 28). The 1920s saw both firms, already profitable, adapting to a new sort of English home market, one where taste was becoming increasingly standardised not just across the classes, but also across the nation, thus allowing manufacturers and retailers to set their sights at much larger areas of population.

Marks & Spencer were alerted to these new possibilities by the success of the American chain store Woolworth's, which opened its first store in Britain in 1909 and by 1919 had eighty-one outlets, including three in suburban London. As one of its founders, Simon Marks noted, his American competitor's rise had been rapid.

> Woolworth's had been making extraordinary progress and were rapidly developing throughout the country. They had become a household word, a great commercial institution. We had marked time and could report no change since the days of my father, other than a few more branches . . . I felt that somehow I had to expand my experience, learn to face up to other people, how to face up to the competition from this commercial giant whose red signs were beginning to dominate the main shopping streets of Great Britain.[19]

Woolworth's was a new type of modern shop, a chain store different in kind from the Victorian and Edwardian department stores which had sprung up to serve the prosperous middle classes. Woolworth's appeal spanned the middle and working classes through the irresistible combination of low prices, good quality and clever psychology: no goods cost more than 6d (figs 29–30). 'Mr Woolworth's success,' commented Thomas Burke, 'is due to his discovery of the fact that millions of people can spend six pence at five different times, or three pence at ten different times, who never at any time

have half a crown to spend. It is irritating to be faced with the proof of a proverb which you don't like and never believed, but these people have proved that if you look after the pence, the pounds will look after themselves.'[20]

It was the example of Woolworth's that caused Simon Marks to visit America in 1924 to study American retail methods. He returned inspired: 'it was about my first serious lesson in the chain store art.'[21] Armed with new techniques of customer psychology, stock control and distribution, he set about transforming his essentially Northern,

28
The Strand, 1930
Photographed by George Reid (1871–1933), this view includes the Strand Corner House, opened in 1915 and the second of Jo Lyons' Corner House restaurants.

29–30
Egg slicer and box
c.1920
9 x 15 cm. Bought in
1921 for 6d at the
Purley branch of
Woolworth's

working-class, nineteenth-century Penny Bazaars into a national chain of modern 'super-stores'. The transformation was sweeping. A five-shilling price limit was introduced in 1928, when the company also adopted its famous green and gold fascia. After incorporation in 1926, the company moved its head office to London. The St Michael trademark was introduced in 1928, and existing stores extended and revamped. New stores were opened, culminating in the company's first Oxford Street store at Marble Arch in 1930.

Marks & Spencer's transformation was not just a matter of public image. The company also revolutionised its internal stock control and, crucially, its relationship with its manufacturers and suppliers. For the first time, at least in England, a retail company took an active role in the internal business of the manufacturer who supplied it, interpreting the state of the market and advising on the production techniques needed in order to guarantee continuous supplies. One of the fields immediately affected by Marks & Spencer's interest in the manufacturing side of their business was the production of cheap clothing for women. New

fabrics such as spun rayon were well suited for factory production, as was the new simplicity of women's clothing – light, serviceable, fashionable yet unfussy. By the 1930s Marks & Spencer's were able to offer complete dresses within its five-shilling price limit.

The invigorated chain stores had an obvious impact on the older department stores, which also looked to American techniques to strengthen their own positions in the market. In the case of Selfridges, this meant an uninhibited resort to spectacular promotions, stunts and publicity coups. Internally, the store was transformed through magnificent new departments, luxurious décor (fig. 31), displays and events. Outside, the shop windows and illuminated decorations grew ever more eye-catching. Selfridges aimed to keep its customers in its store as long as possible, wooing them with amusing things to do. 'In order to show a country friend the attractions of West End shopping,' described one enthusiast:

> I once took her for an entire day to my favourite store. There, besides doing the shopping, we had lunch, tea, wrote several letters in the library, booked seats for a theatre in the evening, telephoned to a restaurant to reserve a table for dinner, 'listened-in' to the wireless programme, read the newspaper in a quiet half hour in the rest room, got a hair cut and manicure and only came out in time to dress for dinner. That is what I call 'making a day of it' at the shops.[22]

Lyons too followed a policy of 'making a day of it' American-style in their establishments. Their Corner House restaurant in Coventry Street near Piccadilly was extended in 1922 to include, amongst

31
Selfridges lift, 1928
Bronze and wrought iron. The panels of the new lifts installed in Selfridges in 1928 were produced by the Birmingham Guild. They were a composite of designs by Edgar Brandt, C.A. Llewelyn Roberts and other metalworkers associated with the Guild.

other things, an all-night café, a food shopping hall, shoe-shine parlour, theatre booking office and telephone bureau.[23] At the more upmarket Trocadero restaurant, cabaret was introduced in 1922 under the keen commercial eye of the theatrical impresario Charles B. Cochran. In 1928 a new, even bigger Corner House opened at the corner of Oxford Street and Tottenham Court Road. This massive establishment served over 21,000 meals in its first day in an astonishingly ornate marble interior decorated with twenty-foot-high murals depicting waterfalls, mountains and woodland scenery. It too provided dancing, bands and everything to make a day of it, including the novelty of the waitresses, the 'Nippies', who since 1926 had been kitted out in smart new black and white uniforms.

However, Lyons' main lesson from America during the 1920s was not the importance of glamour, but the techniques of mass production. And the product the firm transformed as a result was ice cream. Before the war, British ice cream production had been a seasonal effort, undertaken on a small scale, often by Anglo-Italians. By contrast, in America ice cream was produced and consumed far more extensively, and in the early 1920s Lyons engaged an American ice cream expert, Fred Hesse, to build them a prototype ice cream factory. The experiment was successful, and in August 1922 Lyons began to install a massive new ice cream plant in the basement of their Cadby Hall food production premises in west London. The new plant occupied 70,000 square feet, had a production capacity of 50 tons of block ice cream and 100 tons of water ice per day, and was the largest ice cream plant in Europe. Fully operational by 1923, the new plant produced what was sold to the public as American-style ice cream: ready-cut 'bricks' uniform in size and consistency, with a long storage life and produced in hygienic conditions untouched by human hands. All of these qualities added to the product's attraction in the 1920s: American ice cream was clean, efficient and reliable – the ideal treat for modern-minded people. Lyons' experiment was a profitable one, particularly after 1930 when the firm signed a contract to supply Odeon cinemas. In 1920 ice cream consumption in the UK as a whole amounted to three quarters of a

32
Punch,
10 April 1929
Cartoon by Lewis Baumer (1870–1963): 'One used to expect in pictorial advertisements a certain amount of information concerning the article advertised. The modern style, though undoubtedly more arresting, leaves a lot to the imagination.'

33
The Firestone façade, 1929
These fragments from the façade of the Firestone factory were recovered after the demolition of the building in 1971.

million pounds a year. By the outbreak of war in 1939 it had risen to £35.5 million, much of which was being supplied by Lyons.

The visible evidence of American mass production in 1920s London was not just ice cream bricks. The capital's new factories all incorporated the latest American thinking about efficiency, worker psychology and company image. The vast Arcadia Works erected in Hampstead Road, Camden by the Carreras cigarette company was designed in a novelty Egyptian style (see appendix). Outside the entrance stood two massive bronze statues of impassive black cats, said to be the Egyptian goddess Bubatis but conveniently underlining that this was where 'Black Cat' cigarettes were made. A more sober affair was Northcliffe House, a large block erected near Fleet Street, by the *Daily Mail* in 1927 to house a greatly enlarged newspaper operation (see appendix). All the stages of production were gathered together under one roof, from editorial through printing and packing. A more visibly American factory in London was the Firestone factory, the work of English architect, Thomas Wallis, for an American company. Wallis produced an up-to-the-minute efficient building behind an exuberantly jazzy exterior of clashing colour and zigzag patterns (fig. 33). Like Bush House, it brought a flourish of American self-confidence into the London landscape.

Advertising

The invasion of American agencies into Britain brought a totally new approach to copy policy. It might be called 'the psychological revolution'.
R.B. Browne, recalling the 1920s[24]

The 1920s were a seminal period for British advertising. 'Judgment and instinct born of experience,' reflected Ronald Browne, 'were being replaced by science and a new creative process. From being something of an adventure and an art, advertising was becoming a recognised controllable instrument.' Ronald Bousquet Browne had followed his father into the old established agency of T.B. Browne Ltd in 1921 and saw these changes at first hand. Browne's had been established in 1872 and by the time the younger Browne arrived, there were tried and tested house rules. Beneath 'a brief bold headline to attract the reader's interest,' the copywriter would add three things: '(a) a pleasing illustration of the product and/or its use; (b) a bold distinctive nameplate – so that it would be remembered; (c) a brief factual statement in words of the product's purpose and its proven qualities to effect that purpose.' All advertisements were checked to make sure they did not overstep the truth. To the young Browne, this sober approach produced copy that was simple and explanatory but which lacked inspiration.

The revolution that the Americans brought was simply a matter of advertising the results of using the product, rather than the qualities of the product itself. In T.B. Browne's case the agency learned the new lesson when they lost one of their accounts to J. Walter Thompson, an American agency which had recently opened a London office in Bush House. Browne's had been advertising the malted milk drink Horlicks in a straightforward way, reciting its health-giving properties and ingredients. Thompson's adverts depicted a schoolboy whose performance at football miraculously improved when his mother began to feed him Horlicks. The difference in approach was summarised in a 1929 *Punch* cartoon by the artist Lewis Baumer (fig. 32).

Alongside J. Walter Thompson, the other prominent American invaders were the Dorland Agency, whose London office operated alongside offices in New York, Paris, and Buenos Aires, and the agency run by Paul C. Derrick, formerly the marketing director for Ovaltine, who was also the chairman of the American Chamber of Commerce in London throughout the 1920s. Besides a more sophisticated approach to human psychology, the Americans also brought two other new ingredients. The first was 'scientific advertising', the title of an influential book by Claude Hopkins published in 1923 and something of a bible for American advertisers. Scientific advertising championed a

34
Poster, 1920s
152 x 101 cm.
Central image by
P.H. Yorke for a
campaign run by
Benson's advertising
agency. The ethereal
flying woman was a
common motif in
advertisements of
the time.

thoroughly hard-nosed approach on the part of the advertiser, deploying not just the science of psychology but also the sciences of market research, strategic planning and brand imaging. In Hopkins' view, nothing should be left to chance.

The other new element brought by the American advertisers was a kind of religious fervour for the importance of their profession, which they believed was bestowing benefits not just on specific products but on mankind as a whole: advertising drove the world economy, it was 'the industry on which all other industries depend,' it was morally righteous. Something of the zeal of the industry during the twenties was expressed in the speech given by the Prince of Wales at the opening of the twentieth annual convention of the world's advertising clubs which was held at Wembley in 1924 to coincide with the British Empire Exhibition. The Prince declared that advertising was the key to solving all the world's social and economic problems: by enabling a free exchange of commodities throughout the world, peace and harmony would reign; without advertising, there was hardly any function of civilisation that could be carried out at all.[25]

Dissenting views were, of course, expressed. Besides Browne's, the leading older British firms were Mathers & Crowder, established in 1850, and Benson's, established in 1893 by S. H. Benson and taken over by his son Philip in 1914. Philip Benson had visited America to study American agencies and had imported New World ideas into the organisation of his agency. However, he was not altogether sympathetic to either the psychological or the hard-nosed approach.[26] At Benson's the copywriting department was called the 'literary department' and maintained something of a literary atmosphere, producing copy that was humorous, clever and elegant, in sharp contrast to Claude Hopkins' view that nobody with a college education should be allowed to write copy for the mass market. Among Benson's copywriters in the twenties was the young Dorothy L. Sayers whose novel, *Murder Must Advertise*, is set in Pym's Publicity, a thinly disguised Benson's.

Benson's did go in for oblique advertising, most notably in their 1926 campaign for Colman's Mustard which invented a fictional Mustard Club with a cast of quaint characters – The Baron de Beef, Lord Bacon, Miss Di Gester – whose purpose was 'to inspect public sandwiches and report when they contained no mustard.' However, Philip Benson was said to prefer the straightforward approach and his views were vindicated when in 1928 the agency scored a great success with the first campaign for Guinness, built on the old-fashioned approach of simply telling the public that 'Guinness is Good For You'. Mathers also had success with its equally simple slogan for fruit producers in 1923: 'Eat More Fruit'. This campaign was the first instance of a generic campaign promoting a type of food in general rather than a specific product.

If British advertising agencies were not wholly fired up with missionary zeal, neither were British firms, most of whom persisted in seeing advertising as an 'add-on' rather than essential. Confectionery firms were convinced advertisers, as were breweries and tobacco firms, the latter already operating in an international market dominated by the two big conglomerates, British American Tobacco and the Imperial Tobacco Company. One of the smaller British firms was the London-based Ardath Company, producers of State Express cigarettes, a brand heavily promoted in London both before and after the firm's takeover by British American Tobacco in 1925. State Express was a good example of the many twenties tobacco firms who aimed their products at the then new market of women. State Express Eve was Ardath's female-orientated brand and its advertising, like those of its competitors, was designed to associate smoking with women's emancipation and independence. In State Express Eve's case, it did so unambiguously through a trademark of a woman as master-puppeteer manipulating small men on strings (fig. 37). The trademark was made up into a State Express Eve fancy dress which toured charity balls in Britain and Europe where it was said to have won many prizes.[27]

Ardath's also promoted the fine quality of their cigarettes, constantly emphasising that their brands were all hand-made and therefore superior to machine-produced American competitors. For Christmas 1925, Ardath launched presentation 'period caskets' of State Express cigarettes, 'a present every smoker will welcome' (fig. 36). The buyer could choose from eleven types – the Sèvres, Tudor, Princes, Balmoral, de Luxe, Pavlova,

35
Worthington beer advertisement, 1928
W.S. Crawford agency. The text beneath concluded: '... pretty village ... SCHOOL ... change down ... George & Dragon ... nice old pub ... Lunch here? Brakes ... switch off ... TWO WORTHINGTONS, please.'

36–7
Louis cigarette casket, 1925
Eve cigarette box, 1922–5
11 x 14 cm; 8 x 8 cm. Both were made for the Ardath Tobacco Company's State Express range.

Astoria, Sackville, Regal, Golden and the Louis, all of which 'represent an unapproachable niveau of fine quality and appeal to those who will have only the exclusive best.'[28] Cigarette firms were the exception to the rule that British firms were reluctant advertisers, which perhaps helps explain the fact that, as reported proudly in 1928, the British were the greatest smokers in the world with an average tobacco consumption of 3.4 lbs per person.

Advertising raised several variations of the debate about standards and control in British life. Some people called for it to be banned altogether, others thought that untruthful or misleading adverts would disappear of their own accord since they would obviously not survive in the marketplace. In 1926 It Pays to Advertise opened on the London stage, telling the comic tale of a soap manufacturer who had no soap to sell, only a clever advertising campaign. Outdoor advertising was particularly controversial. Were posters and hoardings unsightly eyesores, or were they, as the Prince of Wales proclaimed, 'democracy's Royal Academy' which could raise the artistic taste of the masses? Most people agreed that posters probably should be artistic, but although the generation of artists schooled in Arts and Crafts ideas were enthusiastic about posters' potential for bridging the gap between life and art, the younger generation, with some exceptions, were happy to keep vulgar life at a distance. Advertising agencies were ambivalent. Benson's, for example, had a reputation for outdoor publicity, yet saw the visual element of posters as secondary to the words. At Benson's, the copywriter typed out the copy and put it in an out-tray for someone to illustrate: 'the idea that the artists might have something to contribute to the concept or that something might

come of an exchange of ideas between writer and artist was slow to take root.'[29]

An exception on the agency side was W.S. Crawford's, probably the most progressive of the British agencies. Under their art director Ashley Havindon, Crawford's took a more visual approach to advertising, seeking out novel effects as a way of conveying meaning. Crawford's commitment to art is underlined by their employment in 1927 of Edward McKnight Kauffer. Kauffer, an American who had settled in Britain in 1919, was the one commercial artist whose work was admired by artistic highbrows and who provided something of a bridge between the world of the art gallery and the world of commerce. His work figured prominently in the poster campaigns masterminded by Frank Pick at London Transport and the Empire Marketing Board (see chapter 4).

One of Crawford's most visually arresting campaigns of the late twenties was their 1928 effort for Worthington's beer (fig. 35). It was unusual in using photographs and doubly so for its innovative use of photomontage. This technique was just beginning to make its mark in films of the period, and, interestingly, often in films with a jazz theme. It certainly conveyed the associations of fragmentation and discord that went with the word 'jazz', but also became a useful visual shorthand for the pace and confusion of modern urban life. For the Worthington campaign, Crawford's created a series of these collages, each on a masculine theme – greyhound racing, cabaret, town and country, sporting events, motoring etc. Each carried a piece of equally fragmented text and each placed the bottle of beer as the one reliable and consistent point of calm amidst the frenzy of modern living.

Chapter 3

Russia

Here – one feels at moments – in spite of poverty, stupidity and oppression, is the new Laboratory of Life. Here the chemicals are being mixed in new combinations, and stink and explode. Something – there is just a chance – might come out. And even a chance gives to what is happening in Russia more importance than what is happening in (say) the United States of America.

John Maynard Keynes, 1925[1]

Next to America, Russia was the place whose presence in the world most exercised Londoners during the 1920s. The birth in 1917 of what was to become the Soviet state fascinated and terrified in equal measure. Was the complete reconstruction of a nation's economy and political system on communist principles an act of catastrophic folly or brave idealism? What would be the consequences for the British Empire if the Bolshevik experiment spread elsewhere? A state born of violent revolution rather than slow evolution was particularly threatening and, perhaps inevitably, discussions about Bolshevik Russia were deeply coloured by the language of warfare.

Bolshevism was another invasion; it practised the black arts of propaganda; it was a second Great War – 'having saved civilisation from the Germans and then from the Bolshevik.'[2] Indeed, the 1920s began with Britain formally at war with Russia, as the British government joined the French and Americans in support of the White Russian counter-revolutionaries trying to regain control of the country. The only war artist dispatched to the Russian front for this disastrous and short campaign was Henry Tonks, whose 1919 painting (fig. 38) can perhaps be taken as underlining the popular understanding of Russia as a peasant country several centuries 'behind' England and America.

This chapter looks at two Russian aspects of London during the 1920s. The most important in terms of London's political life was, of course, the impact of Bolshevism, or more precisely, the impact of the fear of Bolshevism. The other prominently Russian ingredient in 1920s London was the ballet. Russian ballet came in two shapes: on the one hand, the *Ballets russes* company under the direction of Serge Diaghilev, which was 'something of a national institution' for twenties London, despite being based in Paris.[3] However, the dancer who had come to embody Russian dancing in London in the years before the First World War was Anna Pavlova. Pavlova had bought a house in London in 1912 and after the war pursued an ever more glittering international career from her base in London.

Can any link be made between the Russian dancers and the Russian revolutionaries, beyond the fact that cartoonists sometimes depicted the Soviet state as 'Mme Bolshova', a ballerina?[4] On the surface these two groups of people and ideas represented quite separate spheres of life, divided not just by areas of activity but also by class and wealth. In London there was also a geographical separation. The Russian ballet operated in the West End theatres and high-bohemian salons of Chelsea

38
***The Surrender of Pujas Gora**, 1919*
Henry Tonks (1862–1937), oil on canvas, 73 x 102 cm.
Tonks depicts the inhabitants of Pujas Gora welcoming Imperial Russian troops who have driven out an occupying force of Bolsheviks.

and Bloomsbury, while Bolshevism belonged to the capital's four 'red boroughs': Battersea, Bethnal Green, Poplar and Stepney.[5] The ballet tended to be associated with the exodus of White Russians who had fled Russia after the revolution and had largely congregated in Paris. There is nothing to suggest that members of the Communist Party of Great Britain had much of an interest in ballet, although they might have made an exception for *Le Pas D'Acier* [The Steel Way], a ballet dramatising sympathetically the Soviet project to transform the Russian economy from a peasant to an industrial one. This ballet had its English premiere at the Princes Theatre in July 1927 and it is said that Diaghilev, wary of possible White Russian protests, sat with a loaded

revolver in case of trouble. In the event the political message of the ballet seems to have passed English critics by and most of the notices concentrated on Prokofiev's powerfully rhythmic music which was damned with faint praise as 'suggesting perfectly the multifarious clanging and motion of modern factory work.'[6]

Despite these obvious differences, there is perhaps common ground between the ballet and Bolshevism in the international mission of both. Art and revolution alike could be transported to any state and dispensed in any language. Both thus brought to London a sense of international awareness quite different from the international awareness that Britain understood from its Empire. The Russian

presence in London was one of many things that reinforced the notion that Britain was now indeed among the nerves of the world, and that catalysts of change were no longer just a matter of the slow evolution of British tradition.

Ballet and Bolshevism also shared common ground in the qualities of emotional expressiveness attributed to both by virtue of their Russian-ness. The popular understanding of the Russian character was that it was peculiarly deep, passionate and soulful, all qualities thought to be thinly spread in the English character. Deep emotional currents ran through the work of the great Russian writers, in particular Tolstoy whose reputation soared in the 1920s. The prima ballerinas Anna Pavlova and Lydia Lopokova constantly reinforced this idea of Russian-ness, not least in their stage performances where both emoted as powerfully as any silent film star. Interestingly, these qualities were also applied to the Bolshevik leaders, Lenin and Trotsky, who were sometimes portrayed even by hostile publications as characters from a Dostoevsky novel, driven by deep passions and a soulful, albeit misguided, spirituality.

Given the quantity of pictures of Lenin and Trotsky that filled the pages of the *Illustrated London News* week after week from 1917 as the gripping tale of Russia unfolded, it is perhaps no surprise that they, like Pavlova, acquired something of a romantic pin-up status. As one jazzily dressed flapper said to another in a Max Beerbohm cartoon of 1920, 'M'dyah, doncher think Trotsky must be *rarther* a darling? Doncher think it would be rarther divine if we had someone like him here? Isn't there something *rarther* touching about him? Of co'rse a Red Terror would be *rarther* awful while it lasted but orl the same, I do think . . .'[7]

39
Anna Pavlova's dress, 1909
Ivan Bilibine (1876–1942), embroidered satin. Designed for Pavlova's first public appearance in London in 1909 in *Danse russe*

Ballet

Early in the summer of 1919 Diaghilev's troupe arrived in London, with La Boutique fantasque *and* Le Tricorne *... imparting, as the Russian Ballet always did, its own culture and collecting its own public, both of which were international. Suddenly the arts became the preoccupation of Society (with the capital S) which twelve months earlier had been preoccupied with military and political intrigue ... Abruptly and unexpectedly the wheels of civilisation began to turn.*

Clive Bell, remembering 1919[8]

The *Ballets russes* had first come to London in 1911 when the company was known as the Imperial Russian Ballet. Pavlova too had first danced in London in 1909 (fig. 39). Then the Russians had been purveyors of exotic, and in the case of the Russian Ballet, excitingly primitive traditions from a faraway land. Their reception after the war was different, not least because of the much changed context from which their work emerged. The revolution had turned the ballet principals into free-floating Europeans, more linked to cities rather than states: Diaghilev made his base in Paris, Pavlova in London. They had also become, as Clive Bell's quote above suggests, more fashionable: in the new High Society salons of the twenties, liking the arts was the modern and interesting thing to do. What precisely then did Russian ballet bring to London in the 1920s? Both Diaghilev and Pavlova did, of course, have a profound influence on the development of British dance and theatre design, an influence that continues to the present day. But they also brought new artistic styles and new ideas, if only through their example, about what it meant to be an artist.

Throughout the 1920s Diaghilev's *Ballets russes* continued to play the role it had before the war of being a channel through which currents of artistic modernism flowed into Britain from elsewhere. Before the war the modernism it brought was the savage, colourful expressionism of the *Rite of Spring*, with its powerful vision of humans stripped back to their primitive core. Diaghilev's productions after the war were less shocking to bourgeois sensibilities but no less impressive to highbrow artistic taste. The 1919 season brought to London some of the heavy-weight modernists of the day, among them Igor Stravinsky, Pablo Picasso and André Dérain. Dérain provided the visual elements in *La Boutique fantasque*. Picasso provided curtains, scenery and costumes for *Le Tricorne*, to music by Manuel de Falla, which had its English premiere at the Alhambra in July. An eloquent reminder of Picasso's stay in London in 1919, the only long visit to the city he made throughout his life, is his portrait drawing of Lydia Lopokova, Diaghilev's star ballerina (fig. 40).

While in London, both Picasso and Dérain were widely admired for moving away from the styles of primitive savagery to a cooler, more ordered classicism. This was a 'civilised' style, deemed to be as universal and expressive as the primitive, but European and post-impressionist in flavour and somehow more suited to English taste. Picasso's classicism found an echo in the work of some of the young English artists who were drawn into Diaghilev's circle during the decade: Christopher Wood's 1926 portrait of the composer Constant Lambert (fig. 41) is a good example. Classical conventions were also reflected in the gold 'Mycenean' masks made by Oliver Messel for Diaghilev's 1925 production of *Zephyr and Flora* at

Picasso
London 1919

40
**Lydia Lopokova,
1919**
Pablo Picasso
(1881–1973),
pencil on card,
36 x 26 cm. One of
several drawings
Picasso made during
the three months he
spent in London in
the summer of 1919
painting sets for
Diaghilev alongside
Vladimir and
Elizabeth Polunin
in their Covent
Garden studio

41
The Composer,
1927
Christopher Wood
(1901–30), oil on
canvas, 57 x 90 cm.
Portrait of Constant
Lambert (1905–51)
who wrote the
music for two
Diaghilev ballets
produced in 1926,
*The Triumph of
Neptune* and
Romeo and Juliet

42–3
Ballet masks, 1925
Oliver Messel
(1904–78). diameter
26 cm. Part of the
muses' costumes in
Zephyr & Flora,
premiered at the
Coliseum in
November 1925.
Designed to be
worn as masks
and, when pushed
up, as hats

the Coliseum (figs 42–3). Messel was still a student at the Slade at the time and this was his first commission for the professional stage.

Although Diaghilev can be seen as an impresario of the highbrow, what makes him particularly interesting is that he also operated in the world of London's commercial theatre. Like Edward McKnight Kauffer, he worked across the gap between art and commerce, seeing no reason to turn his back on the opportunities London's mammoth population offered of a far larger audience than Paris could ever provide. In 1918 he turned to Oswald Stoll of the Coliseum Theatre in St Martin's Lane where dancers from the Diaghilev company appeared on a variety bill, a slightly disconcerting juxtaposition for Harold Acton: 'one had to sit through the antics of jugglers, trick-cyclists and acrobats, before the curtain rose on a single ballet.'[9] More ambitious was *The Sleeping Princess*, a full-length ballet based on the nineteenth-century favourite *The Sleeping Beauty* which premiered at the Alhambra Theatre in Leicester Square in November 1921 (fig. 44).

The Sleeping Princess was an attempt to present a popular spectacle on the lavish scale that the Russian ballet had been famous for before the revolution. It was aimed at a wide audience, and it is said that Diaghilev was inspired by the success of the musical *Chu Chin Chow*, then in its third year at His Majesty's Theatre. The production was extraordinarily expensive, its six sets and three hundred costumes costing well over £20,000. Although *The Sleeping Princess* maintained a modernist edge, in that Tchaikovsky's original music for *The Sleeping Beauty* had been reworked by Stravinsky and the production deployed Diaghilev's trusted team of choreographer Marius Petipa and designer Leon Bakst, the production was generally received by critics as a betrayal of the modernism they had come to

44
Carabosse, the Wicked Fairy, 1921
Leon Bakst (1866–1924), cotton and silk.
Costume designed for Diaghilev's lavish
production of *The Sleeping Princess*, premiered
at the Alhambra Theatre in November 1921

associate with Diaghilev. It was 'scarcely above the
level of a provincial pantomime', full of 'abysmal
commonplaces', 'the suicide of the Russian ballet'
and a deliberate attempt to vulgarise the ballet in the
interests of making money.[10] Audiences displayed
more enthusiasm, but this did not prevent the
production closing prematurely in February 1922,
leaving Diaghilev with a substantial debt.

Diaghilev did not bring another production to
London until 1924 when, in November, *Le Train bleu*
opened at the Coliseum. This time the company
resumed its role as a flag carrier for modernism,
albeit modernism of a very fashionable French sort.
The ballet was set in a smart French beach resort
and was a light and graceful affair with bathing
costumes by Chanel, a scenario by Jean Cocteau and
charmingly acrobatic dancers. Accessible and chic, it
delighted the London critics who declared that this
was 'the new form of the Diaghilev ballet brought to
perfection.' Ballet was once more fashionable and at
Jo Lyons' Trocadero restaurant, Charles B. Cochran
replaced the usual evening cabaret with performances of *Coppelia* every night after dinner.[11]

The French qualities of *Le Train bleu* would also
have delighted the ballet's highbrow followers. The
Bloomsbury group and the circle around the Sitwells
were alike in their Francophilia and their belief that
Paris rather than London was where civilisation's
artistic standards were set. By 1924 the links
between Bloomsbury and the Russian Ballet were
particularly strong thanks to the attachment between
John Maynard Keynes, the Cambridge economist,
and Lydia Lopokova, Diaghilev's star ballerina. The
two married in 1925, finding common ground not
just in their characters but also in their interest in
art. Lopokova was involved in Keynes' short-lived
London Artists Association, an attempt to improve
the economic prospects of visual artists by providing

**45
Lydia Lopokova,
1924**
Frank Dobson
(1888–1963), bronze,
47 x 36 x 35 cm.
The bust is more
fluidly modelled than
Dobson's usually
more stylised
portraits, perhaps
a reflection on
Lopokova's vivacious
character.

privately financed stipends alongside opportunities for exhibiting and selling. Among the several artists helped by the Association was the sculptor Frank Dobson, for whom most of the Bloomsbury coterie sat, including Lopokova (fig. 45).

As Diaghilev worked across the divide between art and commerce, so too did Anna Pavlova (fig. 46). But the art she provided for her 1920s public was of a more traditional and romantic kind. Her art was, she claimed, nothing more nor less than the pure and beautiful expression of the human spirit, a wordless communication of feelings and spirituality. Perhaps reinforced by the new interest in psychology, the notion of dance as a means of expression was an easy one to grasp. It was parodied in a *Punch* cartoon of 1920 where an outbreak of 'Pavlovitis' showed dancers at a charity ball enthusiastically imitating Pavlova's celebrated 'dying swan'.[12] The heroine of James Barrie's 1920 play, *The Truth about the Russian Dancers*, is Karissima, a Russian dancer who only communicates through dance.

Pavlova's first appearance after the war was at Drury Lane in April 1920, an occasion treated by the English press as the return of a great national heroine. Subsequent appearances on the London stage attracted equally rhapsodic coverage, as did reports of her foreign tours and accounts of her home life at Ivy House, Hampstead. Throughout the decade her repertoire was based on dances she had made famous before the war, including her *pièce de résistance*, 'The Dying Swan'. But she also added some new dances, including, in September 1923, a programme of three *Oriental Impressions*, inspired by her recent visit to Asia. Of the three impressionistic dances one was Japanese and two were Hindu in origin, based on Indian folklore and performed in authentic Indian costume to music by an Indian woman composer, Comolata Banerji. In these dances Pavlova was partnered by the Indian dancer Uday Shanker, whose choreography echoed the moves and poses of traditional Indian dance, while also allowing Pavlova to express the 'tragic intensity' of her art, no doubt underlining the point that art was an international language that could be transposed to any cultural setting.

Pavlova's gospel of art as passionate expressiveness went hand in hand with the gospel of art as discipline, hard work and single-minded dedication. She notoriously suffered for her art and this image of the artist as physically and mentally dedicated was also conveyed through press coverage of the various Russian-inspired ballet schools which opened in London in the 1920s. As memorably dramatised in Noel Streatfield's 1936 children's novel *Ballet Shoes*, these schools likewise linked artistic success to discipline and physical training as rigorous as that demanded by any sport. The physical demands of art were echoed in a series of advertisements for the tonic Virol which appeared in October 1926 and featured the Diaghilev dancers Lydia Sokolova and Serge Lifar, 'great artistic personalities [who] live for their art.' Lydia Sokolova had been born Hilda

46
Anna Pavlova,
1924
Photographed
preparing her ballet
shoes in her dressing
room at the
Champs-Elysées
Theatre in Paris

47
Dame Edith
Sitwell, 1927
Pavel Tchelitchew
(1898–1957),
gouache with sand,
63 x 48 cm. The first
of Tchelitchew's
portraits of his
mentor, whom he
had met in Paris
in 1927 through
Gertrude Stein

Munnings and she was among several English or Irish dancers who Russianised or Frenchified their names: Alice Marks became Alicia Markova, Vera Clark became Vera Savina, Patrick Healey Kay became Anton Dolin. This practice was probably little more than the routine adoption of an exotic professional stage name, but also perhaps reflected the notion that if art was a universal language, Russians were particularly well equipped to speak it.

If ballet in 1920s London embodied a Russian mastery of the universal language of art, what about the other art forms? In painting it was France in general and Paris in particular that continued to dominate, many believing with Clive Bell that France's 'standard of civilisation, of intellectual and spiritual activity is higher than that of any other nation.'[13] The sanctification of French art and the canonisation of its principal artists became official with the opening of the 'modern foreign' rooms at the Tate Gallery in 1926.[14] These galleries underlined that there was indeed a relationship between the British school and the French even though both had their own national characteristics, that art could transcend national boundaries and be culturally

specific at the same time. The few Russian painters, stage designers and sculptors who did attract some attention in 1920s London seem to have been read in a similar way, as bringing specific Russian qualitites to a universalist canon. One such was Pavel Tchelitchew, whose works were charged with Russian mystic exoticism yet who also had the impeccable artistic credentials of being based in Paris and being championed by Edith Sitwell. 'Miss Edith Sitwell presents a genius?' was the slightly sceptical heading in *The Graphic* in 1928 above a eulogistic article by Miss Sitwell which made it clear that Tchelitchew's works more than exceeded her highest aesthetic standards: 'we have great and at the first glance slightly terrifying works of art – terrifying because of their silence, of their extraordinary majesty. At first, these paintings have the quality of strangeness. But after a while we become increasingly convinced of their very great beauty.'[15] Tchelitchew executed several portraits of Edith Sitwell (fig. 47), who had fallen violently in love with the Russian in Paris and who continued to champion him even after his emigration to America in the 1930s.

Bolshevism

He is a Red Flag man, he is not a Union Jack Man.
The Daily Telegraph, 1925[16]

If ballet injected an exotic note of internationalism into London's cultural life, Bolshevism was internationalism with a more familiarly British face beneath the mask. Strictly speaking, a Bolshevist was one of the core group of revolutionaries who had overthrown the Russian Tsar in 1917. In twenties London, Bolshevist also took on a wider meaning to embrace anyone awkward, obstreperous and socialist-inclined who supported strikes and militant trade-unionism: anyone who bit the democratic hand that fed them. The story of the Bolshevist impact on 1920s London is thus partly a new chapter in an older British story of industrial and class relations, Bolshevism acting as a sort of distorting mirror through which small fears about the future of the British working classes were magnified to impossibly terrifying proportions. At the same time the association between Russian Bolshevism and the British Labour movement perhaps served to make the alien ideology less frightening. 'Compared with the picturesqueness of the European communist, one finds his English comrade a little disappointing,' said a *Punch* cartoon in 1926 showing a flamboyantly exotic revolutionary standing next to a small man in a raincoat.[17]

The British face of the Bolsheviks was the Communist Party of Great Britain, founded in London on 1 August 1920 (fig. 49). The party had emerged from a chain of events sparked off the previous May when a group of London dockers refused to fuel the Jolly George, a ship laden with arms for the White Russians against the Reds. A number of socialist groups had come together in a 'Hands off Russia' campaign and the foundation of a British communist party marked a more public expression of this left-wing opposition to government policy. British hands were indeed withdrawn from Russia by the autumn of 1920, as the White Russian campaign ran out of steam and British soldiers, already exhausted from battling the forces of evil on the Western front, began to develop distinctly Bolshevist symptoms.

The Communist Party of Great Britain was never a mass movement. In 1929 *The Times* reported that membership was 2000, of which 900 members came from the London district.[18] The party certainly had its base in London, with offices at King Street, Covent Garden, and Great Ormond Street, from where it published an impressive range of journals and newsletters. Although the party had an international outlook, its activities in the 1920s were dominated by events at home. War had left Britain's older industries in a state of chaos, exacerbated by desperate attempts to regain pre-war profitability by cutting wages and increasing productivity (fig. 52). Labour relations in the coal industry in particular deteriorated rapidly, and by 1921 unemployment had begun to spread like an epidemic through the North. Strikes and lock-outs increased in bitterness until the ten-day General Strike of May 1926 brought the country nearer to all out class warfare than it had ever been before.

The General Strike was twenties London's most highly charged event, indelibly associated in many people's minds with the forces of Bolshevism at work in the land, although it grew out of a very British deadlock in the coal industry. On the one hand, the mine owners wished to reduce pay and lengthen hours in order to increase profitability: the

48
Poster, 1921
Dimitri Moor
(1883–1946), 69 ×
106 cm. Entitled
'Long Live the World
Wide Red October',
the poster links the
Russian Revolution
of October 1917
with the victory by
the Red Army over
the allied forces of
America, France,
Britain, Japan and
Czechoslovakia. One
of several Bolshevik
posters acquired by
the British Museum
in 1921.

miners' response was concisely phrased in their slogan 'not a penny off the pay, not a minute on the day'. Support for the miners among other unions produced the call for an all out strike which began at midnight on 3 May 1926. Throughout the ten days of the strike, the government and employers marshalled public volunteers to drive buses, trains and ensure business as usual, with the result that the event turned into a peculiarly British sort of muddling through, rather than a dramatic clash between irreconcilable ideologies. The strike was called off on 12 May with the promise of new proposals for reorganising the coal industry.

The General Strike was a good illustration of the ways Bolshevism and the Labour Movement became inextricably entangled in the twenties. There is no doubt that Britain's most prominent communists had emerged from the Labour Movement: Harry Pollit, for example, a voice of both the Communist Party of Great Britain and the London dockers. But the Communist party also attracted members from more middle-class backgrounds. Francis Meynell, the typographer and antiquarian book-buff, edited *The Communist* in 1921, filling its pages with powerful cartoons by the Australian cartoonist Will Hope, moonlighting from Fleet Street under the pseudonym 'Espoir' (fig. 50). The novelist Graham Greene joined the party in the 1920s, as did the writer Raymond Postgate and the Reverend Conrad Noel, dubbed 'the Red Vicar of Thaksted'. Noel, as reported by the *Illustrated London News* in 1921 with barely disguised outrage, found sanction for Bolshevism in the gospels, hung both the red flag and the Sinn Fein flag in his church, and urged his congregation 'to help the Catholic Crusade to shatter the British Empire, and all other Empires to bits.'[19]

John Maynard Keynes gave a perhaps surprisingly sympathetic reception to communism in his 1925 pamphlet for the Hogarth Press,

A Short View of Russia. As an economist Keynes deplored the economic theory but found far more to admire in the moral vision. 'Leninism is a combination of two things which Europeans have kept for some centuries in different compartments of the soul – religion and business.' Part of the shock for the West, in Keynes' view, was that the business was subordinate to the religion instead of the other way round, but he himself had some sympathy with Lenin's moral world view, particularly when contrasted with its opposite, 'for modern capitalism is absolutely irreligious.' Perhaps, mused Keynes, communism signified a welcome revival of non-materialist values:

It seems clearer every day that the moral problem of our age is concerned with the love of money, with the habitual appeal to the money motive in nine tenths of the activities of life . . . A revolution in our ways of thinking and feeling about money may become the growing purpose of contemporary embodiments of the ideal. Perhaps, therefore, Russian communism does represent the first confused stirrings of a great religion.[20]

The moral streak that Keynes detected in communism is clearly present in Will Hope's cartoons, which deal with matters of right and wrong, particularly within the boundaries of the British Empire. His cartoons tackled incidents which, although not hushed up, tended to be reported in ways that excused British actions. Among the subjects of Hope's cartoons were the Moplah Death Train, where the suppression of a peasant insurrection led to the death of fifty-six Indians by suffocation, and the many Irish deaths that went with the notorious intervention of the 'Black and Tans' (fig. 50). Hope's cartoons pull no punches and illustrate strikingly one of the roles assumed by the communist party during the 1920s which was to voice the minority view that the British Empire was not necessarily always on the side of good against evil.

The same elements of moral drive and stubborn insistence on pointing out an alternative point of view, however unpalatable, can be seen in the career of Shapurji Saklatvala, communist MP for Battersea from 1922–4 and 1924–9.[21] Saklatvala (fig. 51) is another highly charged figure in twenties London. Born in Mumbai (Bombay) in 1874 into a family of merchants and industrialists, he became politicised while working in India for his family firm. Seeing injustice in both British rule in India and the capitalist system, he pursued his political beliefs after moving to England in 1907 through various Marxist and socialist groups, including the Independent Labour Party. It was as organiser of the City of London branch of the Independent Labour Party that Saklatvala began to gain a national reputation, and in 1922 he was adopted as the official Labour candidate for Battersea North, despite having resigned his membership of the Independent Labour Party in 1920 in favour of membership of the communist party.

Battersea at that time was one of London's most radical districts. With a longstanding reputation for independence of thought, it had been the home of the 'Stop the Boer War Committee' in 1900 and regularly refused to fly the Union Jack on Empire Day. In 1913 Battersea had elected London's first black mayor, John Archer. The militant suffragette Charlotte Despard was active in local politics and Battersea had an active branch of the Communist Party of Great Britain. Saklatvala's election in 1922 with a comfortable majority sealed the district's reputation as a 'Little Moscow', 'the nerve centre of the communist movement' and 'the mecca of communism'. Saklatvala remained in Parliament until the 1929 election when the Labour Party finally withdrew its support and he stood as a communist, losing to the Labour candidate.

Saklatvala was a 'one off' in every sense. A communist, a Parsee and a resolute advocate of Home Rule for India, he attracted hostility on every front, as witnessed by the journalist Glyn Roberts in what was probably a fairly typical day for Saklatvala:

50
Cartoon, 1921
Espoir [Will Hope], (fl. 1910–30).
'Ireland: the prisoner was killed whilst trying to escape'

51
Shapurji Saklatvala, 1924
Photographed on the occasion of his fiftieth birthday with his five-year-old daughter Sehri

52
Poster, c.1919
76 x 51 cm. Probably
issued by the
Ministry of Labour
to promote
productivity

I remember, too, staring down at the
Commons from the Visitors' Gallery, hardly
an hour after we had arrived, and wondering
why the sprawling members were so noisy,
rude and unwilling to listen to Mr. Saklatvala
who was endeavouring to speak, through the
nitwit catcalls, loud yawns and irrelevant
interruptions, in connection with the Simon
Report on India, which was the hot news of
the moment, and which was, I imagined in
my ignorance, a subject upon which Mr.
Saklatvala's views, as the only Indian in the
place, might have had some value.'[22]

Saklatvala was also the exception to the rule that
English communists were less picturesque than
their European comrades. Women voters, it was
reported in the 1924 election, seemed particularly
susceptible to some mysterious magnetic force that
he seemed to exude.

Like all communists, Saklatvala came under the
constant attention of a suspicious police force to
whom communists were not a legitimate political
party but an association of seditious people. Like
Catholics before them, communists were suspected
of being part of an international conspiracy with
sinister global ambitions. In the run-up to the
General Strike, the leaders of the Communist
Party of Great Britain had been prosecuted and
imprisoned on charges related to the Incitment to
Mutiny Act of 1797: as historians have pointed out,
an almost unique event in modern British history
of punishment for opinions rather than specific
acts. Saklatvala was himself arrested at the start of
the General Strike, but released when bail was
provided by the East End Labour MP George
Lansbury. In 1928, hearing that the Labour League
of ex-servicemen were to attend a communist
rally in Trafalgar Square to celebrate International
Women's Day, the police superintendents were
instructed to note what was worn, just in case the
demonstrators contravened the Uniforms Act 1894,
which forbade the wearing of anything which
might be confused with official Army dress.[23] In the
event, the men wore 'whip-cord breeches, black
leggings, khaki-coloured drill tunics, Sam Brown
pattern belts, red ties, khaki caps – officers pattern
with scarlet arm bands;' and the women, 'a khaki-
coloured drill overall and red hat, tam o'shanter
pattern.' No arrests were made.

The activities of the Communist Party of Great
Britain were much reported in the papers, but the
anti-Red hysteria was not so much a reaction to
the British communists as to the larger figures of
Trotsky and Lenin that loomed behind them. 'It is
extraordinarily difficult to be fair-minded about
Russia,' said J.M. Keynes, noting that news from
within Russia was likely to be propaganda and
news from without usually came from prejudiced
émigrés.[24] But this did not obscure the very clear

picture presented in most English magazines and newspapers of Russia as a terrible warning of things that might happen here. In this lurid depiction of Russia, the evil Soviet government ruled its people by terror, achieving equality between the classes by pauperising all.[25] In this vision, Russia was also consumed with a passionate hostility towards the British in particular because of their envy of the British Empire (fig. 53). 'Not content with the misery of their own country,' explained the Home Secretary to the House of Commons in March 1927, 'they are seeking to extend that misery to other countries, seeking to destroy civilisation, seeking to destroy what they call the capitalist system. And because we are the head and forefront of civilisation throughout the world, it is the people of Great Britain who have to bear the brunt of the first attack of the Soviet Union.'[26]

Throughout the decade, suspicion of the perfidious Soviet grew ever stronger, fuelled by a succession of incidents. The reopening of trade with Russia in 1920 led to the presence in London of a Russian trade delegation with offices at 49 Moorgate in the City of London. Rumours that the so-called trade delegation was in fact engaged in revolutionary

propaganda came to a head in May 1927 when the police raided the offices of a firm with close connections with the trade delegation, seizing papers and searching the premises. Even more outrageous, at least for Winston Churchill, the incoming Chancellor of the Exchequer in 1924, was the revelation that the Royal Mint had entered into a contract with Soviet Russia to produce silver roubles for the socialist state. Political pressure caused the contract to be cancelled, despite the Mint's arguments that supplying the Soviets was preferable to making workers redundant because of lack of orders. But the most sensational of all the twenties 'red scares' was the infamous Zinoviev letter, the 'red letter' that swayed the results of the October 1924 general election and ensured the fall of the first Labour government, which had come to power only eight months earlier.

The October election had been called so soon after the previous one because of a crisis, itself provoked by a communist scare: the government had dropped charges of sedition against two editors of communist newspapers. In the subsequent furore, the leader of the Labour Party, Ramsay MacDonald, protested that 'I am no communist . . . communism as we know it has nothing practical in

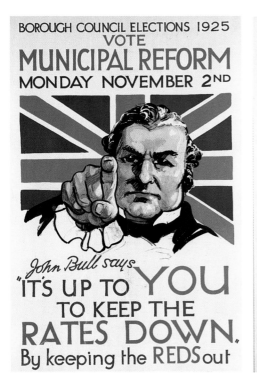

common with us.'[27] But the suspicion remained that his socialist beliefs were somehow delivering Britain into the blood-soaked hands of Lenin. In the election campaign, the Conservatives lost no opportunity to link MacDonald with the colour red. Then, on October 25, the Saturday before election day, 'an election bombshell' appeared, a letter purporting to be from Zinoviev, the President of the international branch of the communist party in Moscow, to the British communist party, instructing party workers to start fomenting revolutionary insurrection immediately among the British working classes. The Foreign Office denied all knowledge of the letter (it was supposed to have been intercepted by their agents); Zinoviev denounced it as an impudent fake, which it subsequently proved to be; but the damage to Labour's electoral chances was done. As Ramsay MacDonald's biographer bitterly remarked: 'If the historian of the future finds the 1924 election interesting on no other grounds . . . he will give it a place as the first in which the methods and discoveries of the new psychology were applied to an ignorant and highly susceptible mass mind.'[28]

Ironically, given the October 1924 election result, political propaganda became one area where Bolshevism could be said to have left its mark on

Britain's culture by encouraging a more visual approach to the communication of political ideas. In Russia, with high rates of illiteracy in the countryside, propaganda relied on strong images to convey meaning. Even their political opponents conceded that this was something Bolsheviks did well: the British Museum acquired a collection of Bolshevik posters in 1921 as examples of modern poster art (fig. 48). British politicians preferred a more straightforward appeal to reason through words (fig. 52). But the 1920s did see a more visual approach emerge, along with a sharper attention to mass psychology. By the 1924 election, not only were posters becoming more visually explicit, but party leaders recorded gramophone messages, took care about how they were presented in the press, and 1924 saw the first-ever election radio broadcasts. One of the effects of this more visual approach to political debate was to semi-demonise the colour red (figs 54–6). It was probably no accident that in January 1924 the *Illustrated London News* should print a lurid picture of a red sunrise alongside its report of the investiture of Ramsay MacDonald as the country's first Labour Prime Minister. According to an astronomical expert, readers learned, the red morn betokened grave disturbances in the weather: 'a red sunrise portends a change for the worse.'[29]

Chapter 4

Britain

The might, dignity, power and prestige of the British Empire are, one and all, symbolised in the Exhibition crest, the lion, designed by Mr F.C. Herrick. The lion is a conventionalised drawing, which brings in all the traditional attributes of the British character – strength, honesty, simplicity.

Official Guide to the British Empire Exhibition, 1924[1]

The British Empire Exhibition of 1924 was one of the defining events of 1920s London. It was a stupendous occasion, the largest exhibition ever held anywhere in the Empire, but to many at the time it also had a stupendous significance. The exhibition promised economic salvation to Britain; it set a new tone to the lines of communication between the separate parts of the imperial whole – nation to nation, state to citizen, manufacturer to consumer; it demonstrated British enterprise not just in the old fields of manufacturing and industry, but also in new arts that ranged from

concrete construction to mass entertainment, advertising to political democracy. Most importantly it was a statement of new ways of thinking about the Empire itself. The British Empire, as redefined by the British government in the 1920s, was not just a relic from Britain's nineteenth-century past but the dynamic key to Britain's twentieth-century future. In the uncertainties of the post-war world, the network of imperial links brought the potential for order.

Empire

Don't buy foreign trash! Buy 'Period' doll furniture. It's British. It isn't patriotic to buy foreign-made toys, especially in these days of the dole.

Toy advertisement, 1923[2]

At its crudest the new idea of Empire promoted in the 1920s was the Empire as a multinational corporation. Global trade was its business. Mutual enrichment was its aim. From being seen as a testament to the military and political superiority of one central nation, the Empire was now redefined as a close, interlocking unit of world trade, a 'common wealth' of separate states that made up a great economic unit on a par with the two other great global economic groups emerging

57
Tea caddy, 1924
13 x10 cm.
Souvenir of the 1924 British Empire Exhibition produced by Lipton's and using the exhibition's official mark, the stylised lion designed by F.C. Herrick

**58
'Empire Made'
merchandise,
c.1930**
Rubber bands made
by H.A. Coombs Ltd
and clearly marked
as British goods

into the post-war world: the United States of America, with a population of nearly 130,000,000, and the combined states of Europe with around 450,000,000. The British Empire was the largest of all with close to 500,000,000 'consumers'. Trade and the generation of wealth had always been at the core of the Empire. However, this new arrangement was in theory supposed to be more equitable for all the constituent parts. The Empire network was exactly like a family, according to the official guide to the British Empire Exhibition. The fundamental purpose of the exhibition was 'to stimulate trade, to strengthen the bonds that bind the mother country to her sister States and Daughter Nations, to bring all into closer touch with the other, to enable all who owe allegiance to the British flag to meet on common ground, and to learn to know each other. It is a Family Party, to which every part of the Empire is invited.'[3]

The Empire Marketing Board, which will appear later in this chapter, also promoted the family metaphor, albeit in a more masculine version of brotherhood through the common experience of work. John Grierson, the film-maker who had begun his career at the Empire Marketing Board, saw the Board's work as giving the new vision of Empire a distinctly socialist flavour: 'for the old flags of exploitation it substitutes the new flags of common labour.'[4] Anti-imperialists would have disagreed profoundly with his view that the old flags of exploitation were no longer flying, but his comment conveys something of the intentions which lay behind the rebranding of the Empire, turning Britain's old territorial spoils into something that felt genuinely more modern and democractic.

What did the British Empire consist of in the 1920s? If it was a family, it was one in which some of the member nations were more privileged than others. At the top of the hierarchy were the Dominions, the self-governing 'white' nations – Canada, Australia, New Zealand, Union of South Africa and, from 1922, the Irish Free State. At the Imperial Conference of 1926 the autonomy of the Dominions was emphasised through the creation of a new subdivision of Empire, the British Commonwealth of Nations, an association of states sharing equal status. Beneath the Dominions were the colonies ruled from London: Kenya, Nigeria and other African states, India, Burma, Singapore, British Guiana and the West Indies. Egypt and Sudan were ruled as 'protectorates', and although Egypt got nominal independence in 1922, the British military presence was maintained because of the strategic importance to Britain of the Suez Canal. The newest arrivals were the 'mandates', those territories awarded to Britain as part of the League of Nations settlement after the First World War. One of the League's first acts was to divide up between the winning nations the colonies of the two losers, Germany and Turkey, thus giving Britain political sovereignty over Tanganyika, the Cameroons, Jordan, Iraq and Palestine. These new additions brought the British Empire to its maximum size of 13,909,782 square miles of the earth's surface, with a population of between 400 and 500 million people.

What did the words 'British' and 'Empire' mean to twenties Londoners? In 1926 the Merchandise Marks Act made it illegal to sell goods without identifying their country of origin and most people had no difficulty transferring the supposed attributes of the British character – honesty,

TROPICAL AFRICAN COLONIES
= IN ACCOUNT WITH =
THE HOME COUNTRY

GOODS WE SOLD	GOODS WE RECEIVED
1895 - £ 2,250,000	1895 - £ 2,000,000
1905 - £ 4,500,000	1905 - £ 3,000,000
1910 - £ 8,750,000	1910 - £ 5,250,000
1915 - £ 9,500,000	1915 - £ 10,500,000
1925 - £ 24,000,000	1925 - £ 20,250,000

GROWING MARKETS FOR OUR GOODS

strength, simplicity – to the world of goods. 'Empire made' and 'British made' became familiar labels (fig. 58), both providing a seal of quality as well as patriotic associations. The idea that British people should 'buy British' had already crept into advertising campaigns well before 1926: 'British cars for British folk', cried the British motor industry in 1925 in an attempt to defend itself from the far cheaper Americans.[5] The oil company Shell, no doubt anticipating similar campaigns in its own field, advertised in July 1925 that as 'a statement of fact . . . more British labour, British capital and British vessels are engaged in Shell than in any other concern dealing in Petroleum products,' by which they meant the Anglo-Persian Oil Company and its distributing arm, British Petroleum.[6] The opening up of the Iraqi oil fields to British commerce

had been one of the main prizes of the post-war land settlements.

If the British Empire and British goods were associated by some with qualities of honesty and strength, to others in 1920s London the outstanding quality of Empire was the political injustice it represented. The promotion of the economic benefits of Empire during the 1920s went hand in hand with increasingly impatient calls for colonial Home Rule, expressed most vociferously in Ireland, Egypt and India (fig. 60). India had been promised a measure of self-government in 1919, but procrastination on the British side and an increasingly powerful nationalist movement on the Indian side, led by the charismatic pacifist Mahatma Ghandi, produced outbreaks of unrest and disturbing events such as the Amritsar Massacre in which

59
Jungles Today Are Gold Mines Tomorrow, 1927
E. McKnight Kauffer (1890–1954), 102 x 305 cm. The central section of a set of posters commissioned by the Empire Marketing Board on the theme 'One Third of the Empire is in the Tropics'

60

Empire cartoon, 1921
'Espoir' [Will Hope], (fl. 1910–30). Printed in
The Communist in June following the unveiling
in London of a statue of George Washington,
the one-time leader of a colonial revolt against
British rule: 'It now only remains to compel the
ungrateful Indian, Egyptian and Irishman to join
the British Empire in honouring the principles
set forth in the Declaration of Independence.'

unarmed supporters of Indian self-government
were killed by British troops.

Throughout the 1920s Home Rule movements
also began to find a voice in London itself through
the emergence of groups and societies such as the
African Progress Union, founded in 1918 under
the presidency of the remarkable John Archer, the
West African Students Union formed in 1925, and
the India Freedom Association, formed in 1925 with
the motto 'Freedom within the Empire if possible –
outside if necessary'.[7] These groups acted in part as
social networks, helping people find their feet in
what was sometimes a hostile city, but also became
forums for the discussion of ideas about the progress
of nationhood in India, Africa and Britain's other
'black' colonies. The radical direction in which
many of these groups went was perhaps inevitable
given the very obvious gap between the rhetoric
of the British Empire, which trumpeted values of
freedom and justice, and the actual experience of
both black African nations and black individuals in
London. A source of particular hurt was the British
government's refusal in 1919 to allow colonial
troops to take part in the main Victory March.

The emerging arguments about African
nationalism were given a more public hearing
through the two Pan-African Congresses which took
place in London during the decade. The first such
congress had been held in Paris in 1919, but in
1921 and 1923 sessions were also held in London.
The 1921 congress produced a radical 'London
declaration' which openly criticised the British
Empire, not just for 'denying its coloured colonies
the rights of self-government which it freely
gives to white men,' but, more crucially, of
failing to encourage any movements towards self-
determination by putting mechanisms in place to
train and empower black men and women to play a

61
HRH The Prince of Wales, 1925
John St Helier Lander (1869–1944), oil on canvas, 112 x 87 cm. Entitled 'Royal Friends' by the *Illustrated London News* whose 1924 photograph of the Prince at Biarritz was the basis of the painting

role in their country's future government. The fuel that drove these Home Rule arguments was moral as well as political outrage, not just at the fact of the Empire's inequitable distribution of human rights, but also at the rhetoric which presented the Empire as one big happy family.

To most Londoners, the idea of the Empire as one large family where differences between national peoples were only a matter of skin colour and dress was embodied by the Prince of Wales, the eldest son of George V and later to be crowned as Edward VIII. Throughout most of the decade, the Prince acted as 'our roving ambassador', touring the world on official visits, from India to South Africa, combining in his one person the constitutional ties which bound the Empire together, the traditional attributes of the British character with its modern democratic incarnation. He was very much a man of the modern age; newspapers reported him surfing in Hawaii, playing polo, frolicking in the on-board swimming pool on HMS Renown or posing for the camera in fancy dress – even, on one occasion, in drag.[8] On his overseas visits, the Prince often donned some traditional article of clothing from his host country, behaviour that historians have interpreted as projecting a subliminal message that Empire citizens were all the same beneath their dress.[9]

A 1925 portrait of the Prince (fig. 61) shows him as an informal modern royal, dressed distinctly unstuffily and clutching his favourite dog which he had raised from birth, hence the title *Royal Friends*. The picture was painted by John St Helier Lander directly from a photograph printed in the *Illustrated London News* in April 1924 showing the Prince at Biarritz recuperating after breaking his arm at polo.[10] This was the second such picture St Helier

Lander had painted from a magazine photograph. The first was a full-length portrait showing a sporty Prince dressed to play polo. Both works had been commissioned by the *Illustrated London News* and both were donated to provincial art galleries after serving as colour reproductions in the magazine.[11] The Prince of Wales was not the face of the Empire that the rather more sober Empire Marketing Board chose to promote, but his celebrity status in newspapers and magazines meant that he, rather than his father George V, assumed the role of head of the Empire family during the twenties.

Exhibition

Never since the human race drew breath upon this planet did men hold such a gathering from over land and sea with plan and purpose for the bettering of mankind.
The Archbishop of Canterbury, 1924[12]

The idea of a great exhibition to celebrate the Empire had been conceived as far back as 1913. At that time the model was the great commercial exhibitions on imperial themes mounted by Imre Kiralfy at the White City from 1902. Like Kiralfy's shows, the original 1913 proposal was a private initiative, in this case devised by two limited companies, the British Dominions Exhibition Ltd and the Great London Exhibitions Ltd. Where the 1924 exhibition as eventually realised departed from its 1913 conception was the active involvement of the British government. Although the Kiralfy exhibitions had communicated ideas about Britain and its empires, the 1924 exhibition was the first time these ideas had come with the explicit approval of the state. The British Empire Exhibition can thus be seen as one of twentieth-

62
Silk headscarf,
1924
The souvenir depicts
the main buildings at
the British Empire
Exhibition.

century Britain's first great experiments in state-sponsored 'peacetime propaganda'.

The involvement of the state in such an enterprise was originally limited to the role of guarantor. In 1920 the government agreed to underwrite the exhibition to the sum of £1.5 million. Doubts were expressed then about the legitimacy of public money being used to assist 'purely business propaganda', but in 1922 the government announced that it would not only underwrite the whole enterprise, it would also actively participate with displays of its own. The reason, according to the government's final evaluation of its involvement, was in part the wish to publicise

'the main activities of His Majesty's Government, the existence of which were completely unknown to the public who benefited by them.'[13] In an age of mass democracy, mass psychology and a state increasingly concerned with domestic matters, it was only really a matter of time before the government turned its attention to presenting itself to the public.

The site chosen for this great undertaking was Wembley Park in northwest London. The location was criticised by some for being too far out of town, but in fact provided both a vast space for the buildings and good public transport: the site was served by two railway lines which meant that

63
Imperial Stadium Choir, 1925
Formed in 1924, the choir performed in all the exhibition's major ceremonies. Here they are photographed in the Cockney costumes they wore in the 1925 Torchlight and Searchlight Tattoo.

over a hundred stations in the London area were within eighteen minutes journey time.[14] Public transport was further improved for the exhibition by erecting what *The Times* called a 'motor-omnibus station' designed for over 100,000 passengers a day, with buses departing every fifteen minutes as directed by the electronic indicator boards. The bus station was, reported *The Times*, the first of its kind to be built in the world and had 'excited so much interest in transportation circles that telegraphed enquiries have been received in regard to it from New York, Chicago and San Francisco.'[15] The Prince of Wales agreed to become patron and declared that he attached immense importance to the project, not least because the scheme included the erection of a great imperial stadium, suitable as the home of every form of British sport.

The whole massive exhibition enterprise began in January 1922 with the construction of Wembley Stadium, which was completed in time to house the 1923 Football Association Cup final. The event attracted thousands of spectators, many of whom famously invaded the pitch at the end of the match. The site as a whole was even more gigantic. In addition to the stadium and the bus station, the elements to be erected included hundreds of buildings, an amusement park, an ornamental lake, a new reservoir, new outfall sewer, new railway lines and roads, all spread over a site the size of six

Trafalgar squares and all built from the then wonderful new material – concrete.

Concrete was used, according to the architects John and Maxwell Simpson, for reasons of economy and speed. Concrete construction technologies were rapidly developing in America, and concrete, along with rayon and aluminium, had distinctly modern associations. As the Concrete Utilities Bureau advertised:

The day is approaching when we shall as a general rule live in concrete houses, walk on concrete pavements, ride over concrete roads, find our way by means of concrete road signs, conduct our business in concrete offices, carry out our manufactories in concrete factories, draw our water from concrete reservoirs, conduct it through concrete pipes, carry away our sewage in concrete sewers, and, finally, have our epitaphs inscribed on concrete monuments.[16]

The exhibition fulfilled most of this prophecy. Not only were the exhibition buildings themselves made of concrete, but also all the street furniture – lamp posts, flag poles, ornamental statues, drinking fountains and amusement bridges. The six massive statues of lions that sat outside the government building

64
**Commemorative
stamps, 1924**
For the 1924
exhibition, Harold
Nelson designed
Britain's first
commemorative
stamps: 1d red
and 1½d brown.
The stamps were
reissued in 1925.

**65–71
Wembley
souvenirs, 1924–5**
Max. height, 16 cm.
The blue jar was
made by the
Newport Pottery,
Staffordshire. The
other makers are
not known. The cat
motif may refer to
the British Gas
exhibit in the Palace
of Industry where
visitors were
instructed: 'be
sure you stroke
the lucky cat.'

symbolising the power and dignity of Empire
were made of concrete, and the Palace of
Engineering was said to be the largest concrete
building in the world.

Concrete was not the only example of British
modernity demonstrated by the exhibition. The
opening of the exhibition on 23 April 1924
(St George's Day) provided the occasion for the
first words spoken by a British sovereign to his
people and the world at large by radio. The words
were no more than to declare the exhibition open,
but they were flashed around the world, received
at the telegraph office on the Wembley site and
delivered back to the King by a telegraph delivery
boy eighty seconds later. King George V was also
involved in another Wembley innovation – the first
issue by the General Post Office of pictorial stamps
(fig. 64).[17] Until 1924 British stamps had never
deviated from their nineteenth-century template
showing just the monarch's head. The idea of a
new design was mildly controversial, and the King
at first expressed himself 'not very much in favour
of stamps of this sort because the whole idea is
un-English and is copied from America.' Nevertheless the project proceeded and designs were
invited from a number of distinguished artists,
including Eric Gill, whose designs were rejected
by the King in favour of the more traditional
design produced by Harold Nelson. To great public
irritation, the new stamps were only available at
the Post Office on the Wembley site. The General
Post Office's impeccably logical explanation was

that the stamps had been issued for the sole
purpose of attracting people to the Wembley site, a
function they could not fulfil if they were available
everywhere.

The site's main focus was its buildings and pavilions
erected to represent the countries of Empire (fig. 62).
There were sixteen of these, ranging in size from
Australia, which was housed in a enormous 'palace',
to the smaller West Indies/British Guiana building
which housed a cocktail bar and displays on sugar.
Although most of the general exhibition buildings
were constructed from concrete, the national pavilions
presented a mix of different architectures. The West
African building was a miniature reproduction of the
walled city of Zaria in Nigeria; Ceylon was modelled
on the Temple of the Tooth in Kandy; Burma
reproduced in Burmese teak one of the gates of
a famous pagoda at Mandalay. Hong Kong was
represented by a street of Chinese shops, and East
Africa by a white-walled Arab building. Inside visitors
saw educational demonstrations, native art and
manufactured goods and products. The Australian
pavilion sold seven million apples and had to send
for more. The Canadian pavilion promoted its dairy
products with a refrigerated, life-size sculpture of the
Prince of Wales in butter. For the 1925 season, they
topped this with a life-size butter sculpture of the
Prince of Wales in the costume of a Red Indian chief.

What about the displays in the British Government
building? This experiment in publicity comprised
an enormous variety of exhibits covering every
government department from the Public Record

Office to the Department of Overseas Settlement. The Department of Overseas Trade contributed a massive map of the world with electronically lit shipping routes; it was subject to constant breakdown 'owing to children tampering with the model'.[18] The Ministry of Health had a model of sewage disposal. The War Office exhibited models of battleships and a 'Court of Honour' which extolled the heroism of famous men such as Nelson and Scott of the Antarctic alongside ordinary British types such as Tommy Atkins (a soldier), a policeman and a fireman. The General Post Office exhibited a working model of a recently installed automatic telephone exchange which was said to be among the most popular exhibits. The building also included a theatre, where the Admiralty staged recreations of famous naval battles, and a cinema which showed sixty-three films made by various government departments, including such titles as 'Three Million Letters a Day', 'A Loaf of Bread' and 'Clean Milk'. These presentations, it was reported, were not popular and were put in the shade by the success of 'Zeebruge' playing in the theatre next door. Also popular was the theatrical production of 'London Defended', the War Office's dramatisation of the arguments for a civil air defence system.

Government activities also extended into the stadium events, notably the 'pageant of Empire', the object of which 'was a frankly imperial one: to pay tribute to those qualities which have brought about the expansion throughout the world of the British race.' As originally conceived, the pageant took a historical and linear approach to the story of Empire, thereby underlining Britain's central role. This was objected to by the Dominions, who wanted a geographical rather than a historical structure, and after much dispute, and the resignation from the organising committee of Rudyard Kipling, the matter was resolved as a compromise in three parts –

The Dawn of Empire, The Empire's Growth, and Southward Ho! The pageant employed 15,000 largely amateur performers, 12,000 historic costumes and massed choirs, and the result was agreed by the press to be a spectacular testament to British heroism, endeavour and pride.

The British Empire Exhibition ran initially from April to November 1924. But it was considered such a success that it was decided to run a second season in 1925. In terms of visitor numbers, the exhibition was a triumph: bank holiday Monday in May 1924 attracted a record daily total of 300,000 people. By July 6.5 million people had visited and the amusement park, where individual rides charged extra admission fees, was taking thousands of pounds a day. Souvenirs proved lucrative too, particularly for those pottery firms who kept their costs low by re-using old shapes and designs, adding only a glossy coloured glaze or new pattern to bring them superficially up to date (figs 65–71). Many of the products on sale at the exhibition drove design pundits to despair.

By the end of the season, the visitor total had risen to an estimated ten million, among whom were various foreign kings and queens. These included His Imperial Highness Ras Tafari, the heir apparent to the Abyssinian throne whose visit to London in July

72
Diana (from
Lionel and
Clarissa), c.1924
Gwendolyn Parnell
(fl. 1914–36), height
20 cm. Originally
a portrait painter,
Parnell took up
figure modelling in
1914 to provide a
British replacement
for German
porcelain figures.

1924 attracted much press attention, not least because this was said to be the first occasion on which the mysterious prince had ever left his equally mysterious kingdom. The exhibition had been promoted as the world in miniature, and the visit of Ras Tafari seemed to confirm that all human life was indeed there in 1924 in a suburb of North London.

Marketing

The one great piece of Imperial publicity that has been organised – the Wembley Exhibition – was, as propaganda for the British Empire, a colossal world-wide success ... but an Imperial Publicity Bureau, when one thinks about its opportunities, might well send us soaring into the greatest period of prosperity that Britishers have ever known.
Charles Higham, 1925[19]

For traditionalists, publicity and marketing were activities in which the state had no business getting involved. For modernisers, like Sir Charles Higham, 'all that advertising has done for the popularisation and sale of merchandise it can do for the popularisation and dissemination of ideas.'[20] Government must turn its attention to the moulding of public opinion, particularly when public opinion formed a 'mysterious tyrannical obstruction' to progress. In his 1925 book Higham

noted that only seven government departments employed publicity officers and none of those seven had any training in direct advertising. He was particularly critical of the General Post Office whose dilatory approach to the public amounted to 'some tentative telephone advertisements and a few admirable signs.' By using modern methods of suggestion, Higham predicted, 'the state can make the telephone as much a part of the equipment of any ordinary home as the front door or the roof.'

The 1920s saw several state-associated experiments in influencing public opinion. The Wembley exhibition was something of an exception in its success with the public. Others were more tentative, concerned as much with finding administrative models for this unprecedented use of public money as with the nature of their messages about Britain and Britishness. A good example is the British Institute of Industrial Arts (BIIA) established in 1919 with the aid of a grant from the Board of Trade. This initiative had first been suggested before the war, when it had been deemed to 'go beyond the proper limits of state action,'[21] but it was revised after the war and the Institute allocated a small grant to establish an exhibition of British design in Knightsbridge. The state had been trying to improve the artistic quality of British products since the mid-nineteenth century through the technical education systems established by the Science and Art department of the Board of Education. What made the BIIA different in kind from its predecessors was that it was an attempt to influence the purchasers of British products rather than the producers. Instead of trying to encourage manufacturers to produce 'good' British design in abstract, a strategy that to some was demonstrably futile, the new Institute would try and create an informed, design-conscious public whose demands British manufacturers would find irresistible.

The BIIA's exhibition was set up in 1920 and greeted with rapturous enthusiasm by the *Illustrated London News* whose writer pursued a curious electrical metaphor throughout his report. The Institute was to be 'a Power station of British Craftsmanship' and 'the switch board for connecting the William Morris of the future with the factories and markets.'[22] The exhibits included factory-produced products, such as Poole pottery and Whitefriars glass, alongside the work of the small crafts studios which had begun to flourish in London after the war. Charles Vyse and Gwendolyn Parnell were typical of this new brand of 'designer makers'. Both had potteries in arty but fashionable Chelsea, and both aimed their work at a smart metropolitan clientele (figs 72–3). Though well received critically, the BIIA's initial exhibition failed to inspire the public, and following the withdrawal of the Board of Trade's funding, the Institute limped on through the 1920s with a series of reports and temporary exhibitions ('British Industrial Art for the Slender Purse' in 1929) to be finally wound up in 1933. It left a lasting legacy in its permanent collection of objects, transferred to the Victoria and Albert Museum on the Institute's closure, and in its basic idea of government-sponsored design promotion which resurfaced in various forms throughout the century, evolving finally into today's Design Council.

A more ambitious government attempt to influence consumer choice was the Empire Marketing Board, founded in 1926 as a body attached to the Dominion Office.[23] It had no constitutional precedent and was charged with spending its generous grant of public money on promoting Empire goods and products at the expense of foreign. Like a commercial advertising agency, it was organised in three sections –

publicity, marketing and research – but the Board were at pains to distance themselves from their commercial counterparts:

No government, except perhaps in wartime, has ever embarked upon so large a publicity campaign as this. Moreover, both the spirit and form of the publicity required are novel and cannot follow closely any ordinary commercial model. Much exploratory and experimental work will plainly be required before effective publicity of the quality needed can be organised in the many fields indicated.[24]

The Publicity Committee's poster campaign was the most visible result of the Empire Marketing Board's activity. By 1931, when the poster campaign began to be wound down, over eight hundred posters on the theme of Empire had been commissioned, produced and reproduced for display on a thousand hoardings up and down the country. All had been tightly controlled down to the last detail by the Publicity Committee under its dominant chairman, Frank Pick, then Managing Director of the London General Omnibus and Underground groups. Pick was already responsible for one of the two commercial precedents that cannot help but to have informed the Board's poster work. The posters he himself commissioned for his tube and bus companies were, by

74–5
Sorting Manganese Ore, 1928
Gathering Cocoa Pods, 1928
Gerald Spencer Pryse (1882–1956), 102 x 305 cm. Two panels from the set, 'What Gold Coast Prosperity Means', completed after Pryse had persuaded the Empire Marketing Board to finance a tour to West Africa to see his subjects at first hand.

general agreement, the perfect balance between good art and public usefulness. The other precedent was a purely commercial initiative from the British Empire Exhibition which in 1923 had commissioned the artist Gerald Spencer Pryse to produce fifteen large lithographs showing life and labour in Empire countries. Reportedly inspired by the Prince of Wales' speech about posters being democracy's Royal Academy, the lithographs were produced as large posters, but also in smaller sizes and sold through the *Illustrated London News*.[25] Like Frank Brangwyn, whose style his own resembled, Spencer Pryse was an artist of the Arts and Crafts generation who welcomed the chance to design for the mass market: 'He does not believe in art for arts sake,' reported the *Illustrated London News*. 'No such detachment is possible.'

Pryse was one of many artists commissioned by the Empire Marketing Board to produce their own posters (figs 74–5). The minutes of the Publicity Committee reveal the laborious nature of the commissioning process as Pick rigorously exerted quality control over every detail of image, text and approach.[26] Official government posters, it was felt, had to maintain 'higher' standards than those applied to commercial posters: they had to educate as well as sell. Thus, the Board's posters were displayed on specially designed hoardings on 'solus' or single sites to mark them out from the mass of commercial advertising, and the posters themselves displayed a patrician visual dignity by generally separating the image from its often ponderous accompanying text. The artists commissioned by the Board tended to be those who matched Pick's views about art, which tended towards the highbrow. Pick preferred work to be disciplined and tidy but also clean and modern, a combination well illustrated by one of his favourite artists, Edward McKnight Kauffer (fig. 59). He was not altogether happy with Spencer Pryse but perhaps

felt that as an artist with an established interest in Empire labour, he could not be left out. Artistic merit was the grounds on which he rejected a recommendation from the Governor of Nyasaland that a local artist be used for an East African poster. One of the few commissioned artists with substantial links to the place being depicted was the Burmese artist U Ba Nyan who produced a set on the theme of 'Burmah, a Land of Rich Resources' in 1928 (fig. 76).

The reconciliation of education and commerce was one of the Empire Marketing Board's failures, or so concluded 'Philistine', who reviewed their exhibition of posters at the Royal Academy in 1926 for the trade journal *Advertising Display*.[27] Philistine had misgivings about posters which bore no lettering at all and wondered about the Board's artistic policy, which ruled out more obviously realistic and therefore populist images. He also wondered whether enough thought had gone into the message: 'the present appeal is to patriotism; to one's almost purely disinterested desire for the welfare of the Empire as a whole. It would be libellous to say that such an appeal is of no avail . . . [but] the patriotic appeal will need to be supported by a frankly commercial one.' The question of commercial effectiveness was also raised in an internal report following up the dispatch of ready-printed display materials to 3000 grocers in London during 1928.[28] The Board's inspector found to his dismay that some of the shopkeepers ignored the material completely and others misused it: the Board's Irish butter poster showing an Irish wolf hound was found in one shop 'with a Spratt's Dog Biscuit advertisement carefully pasted to the bottom.'

The supply of display materials to shops was one of several other activities that the Publicity Committee developed. It collaborated with the Advertising Association to organise an Empire Display Week in London in July 1927: 'for one week London's shop

76
A Paddy Field,
1928
U Ba Nyan
(1897–1945), 102 x
305 cm. One panel
from a set on the
theme: 'Burmah:
A Land of Rich
Resources'. An
artist from Myanmar
(formerly Burma),
Nyan studied art in
London and later
taught at the Royal
College of Art.

windows will be one vast Imperial advert . . . we shall see that all the goods and produce we need can be obtained within the bounds of the great British Commonwealth of Nations.' It reprinted its posters at a small size for sale to schools – a very successful initiative which resulted in over 200,000 posters being sent to over 20,000 schools. It took stalls at exhibitions such as at the Ideal Home exhibition in 1927 where it showed a five-room bungalow stocked entirely with Empire products and designed to demonstrate how the use of Empire goods would also help 'transform the house-drudge into the chic Eton-cropped housewife.' In the wake of the Merchandise Marks Act of 1926, the Committee also asked Edward McKnight Kauffer to design a 'National Mark' which could be used across the board to brand British goods. The project never got further than the prototype stage and in many ways was rendered unnecessary by the fact that many manufacturers considered that a National Mark already existed in the form of the Union Jack.

More longlasting was the Board's interest in film, thanks to the employment in 1927 of John Grierson to head the Empire Marketing Board's new film unit. Grierson's first film for the Board, *Drifters* (1929), an elegiac account of North Sea herring

trawlers described by Grierson as a declaration of faith in the beauty of common life, is generally acknowledged as marking the start of English documentary film. Interestingly for a promoter of Britishness, Grierson had been much influenced by Soviet film and was instrumental in the first showing in London in 1925 of Eisenstein's hitherto banned *Battleship Potemkin*. After the Empire Marketing Board was disbanded in 1933, he transferred to the newly formed General Post Office film unit where he presided over a series of poetic documentaries about working life, raising new ideas about what it meant to be British.

Grierson's claim (quoted on p. 68) that the Empire Marketing Board's image of the British Empire was a non-exploitative one is difficult to agree with in the twenty-first century. Now it is less easy to ignore the undertones of economic exploitation that are undoubtedly present in some of these eighty-year-old posters. But taken as historical documents from a particular time, the posters do mark an attempt to dignify the idea of Empire through connecting the various peoples of Empire to supposedly shared common values, and – crucially – values that sprang from the field, factory floor and workplace rather than the palace or government office.

Chapter 5

England

The sounds of England, the tinkle of the hammer on the anvil in the country smithy, the corncrake on a dewy morning, the sound of the scythe against the whetstone, and the sight of a plough team coming over the brow of a hill, the sight that has been seen in England since England was a land, and may be seen in England long after the Empire has perished ... These things strike down into the very depths of our nature, and touch chords that go back to the beginning of time and the human race.

Stanley Baldwin, 1924[1]

If Britain stood for the public qualities of honesty and fair dealing that were supposed to underpin the Empire, what did England stand for in twenties London? Stanley Baldwin's famous 1924 eulogy on Englishness encapsulates much of it. England stood for the essential spiritual values carried in the soul, the timeless bond between mankind and nature – a bond that transcended any one political system, the sense of individual identity through sensory pleasures. England stood for the private and intimate, the spiritual and the primitive; it was sensed in the country rather than the city. Whereas Britain was the Tudor galleons that had set sail to make the Empire, England was the plough and the cottage.

London was, of course, the one place where Englishness was thought to be virtually extinct. To London's critics, urbanisation, globalisation and mechanised production had long since cut any links to the natural world and erased any sense of spiritual values: London's fog was also 'the drab fog of colourless cosmopolitanism'.[2] However, Englishness was a recognisable thread in the ideological tapestry of twenties London, not least in superficial ways as a design style that looked to the English past: 'the taste for Tudor' and mock Georgian being the most popular examples. Historicism in design was no new

phenomenon of the twenties. Ever since William Morris and the Arts and Crafts movement had canonised the craftsman, manufacturers had been falling over themselves to link their products to the artistic superiority of the hand-made. By the twenties, such ideas had become mainstream and London's furnishing shops were full of Jacobean gate-leg tables, Tudor sideboards, Georgian oak panelling and Elizabethan casement windows. Wholly mechanically produced pressed glass was sold to the public under the trademark names 'Jacobean' and 'Chippendale'; the ubiquitous 'Tudor' appeared on products as diverse as toffees and batteries.

A more profound sense of Englishness was also to be found in London in the work of those artists who consciously saw themselves working within uniquely English traditions. The Society of Wood Engravers, formed in London in 1920, and its offshoot, the English Wood Engraving Society, included the majority of the decade's most self-consciously 'English' artists, Paul Nash, Leon Underwood and Robert Gibbings among them. But the artist most celebrated during the decade for his English qualities was the sculptor Eric Gill. A typical review from *The Times* in 1929 announced with pride that Gill's work constituted 'a native

77
The Kinlog, 1927
Kathleen M. Milnes (d.1943), 55 x 40 cm.
The 600-page Kinlog was begun in 1927 as the
annals or official history of the Kibbo Kift. The
figures shown on this page are the semi-mythical
English heroes, Wayland Smith and Robin Hood.

talent in native materials which can hold its own with anything in Europe. All the more secure because the talent really is native, developing on its own lines and owing practically nothing to the post-Rodin convention in sculpture which is quite legitimately being pursued in all countries.'[3] Despite his Roman Catholicism, Gill came to be widely understood as an archetypally English artist: his craftsmanship, use of local stone, spirituality, sense of the past and otherworldly eccentricity in dress all paralleling the Baldwin vision of Englishness as a semi-mystical communion with nature and history. What was, of course, less appreciated at the time was the degree to which Gill's reverence for the sensual pleasures of the physical world went far further, sexually, than anything Baldwin might have understood as typically English behaviour.

Far less well known than Eric Gill but an equally fascinating mixture of conventional and unconventional Englishness during the twenties is the group who form the subject of this chapter: the Kindred of the Kibbo Kift (fig. 78). The Kibbo Kift took their name from old English dialect words meaning 'trial of great strength', and their Englishness took a particularly intense and assertive form. They are interesting to look at not because they were in any way representative of the mainstream – like Eric Gill, their vision of Englishness included a physical primitivism that Stanley Baldwin would probably have found alarming – but because they were arguably 'the only genuine English national movement of modern times',[4] an attempt to reassert a sense of national identity in the chaotic internationalism of the post-First World War world. Or as they themselves put it: 'Since the Kindred has forged itself in England, it says, "Come on, England! Be England – by ash, and oak, and thorn!"'[5]

78
**The Kindred of
the Kibbo Kift,
1928**
The founder
John Hargrave
(1894–1982) is in
the third row,
third from right.

Kibbo Kift

*Mass inertia is only overcome by the energy of
the Few.*

John Hargrave, 1927[6]

The Kindred of the Kibbo Kift was formed at a
meeting in Denison Hall, Vauxhall Bridge Road on
18 August 1920, and its aims set down in the form
of a seven-point covenant:

1. Open air education for the Children.
   Camp training and nature craft.
2. Health of Body, Mind and Spirit.
3. Craft training Groups and Craft Guilds.
4. The Woodcraft Family, or Roof Tree.
5. Local Folk moots & Cultural Development.
6. Disarmament of nations – Brotherhood
   of Man.
7. International Education based on these
   points. Freedom of Trade between Nations.
   Stabilisation of the Purchasing Power of
   Money in All countries. Open Negotiations
   instead of secret treaties and diplomacy.
   A World Council.

Later tweakings modified the words but essentially
the double focus of the Kindred's mission remained
in place throughout the 1920s. On the one hand it
aimed to develop the physical and mental health of
the individual through natural pursuits: 'the Kindred
began as a body impulse to get Earth contact in a
mechanical age.'[7] On the other it campaigned for
its big Utopian vision of international concord
above and beyond the nation state: 'The kindred
exists to enter into the everyday life of the people
of the earth, sending roots into their most vital
regional traditions and feelings, in order to combat
Nonentity. It stands for This Particular Man on
this Earth as against Nemo the "national" of The
Nonesuch State.'[8]

The double focus of the Kindred's work reflected
the double focus of John Hargrave (1894–1982),
the movement's twenty-six-year-old founder,
whose two defining experiences in life up to 1920
had been the Scout movement and the First World
War. Hargrave's central importance to the Kibbo
Kift cannot be over-emphasised. He was the
movement's Head Man, Inspirator, 'the Great
Doer', 'The Word Slayer' and unchallenged leader.
A man of scorchingly strong charisma, he looked,

79
John Hargrave,
1927
Photographed at the
Gleemote gathering

80
Totem of Angus
Og, 1927
Height 36 cm. The
wooden totem of
'Angus Og', Kin
name of the
photographer Angus
McBean (1904–90)

according to one awe-struck acolyte, like Mephistopheles with a Byronic air (fig. 79).[9] Hargrave was born into a Quaker family, and after a seminomadic existence moving between the Home Counties and the Lake District, the Hargraves settled in Buckinghamshire, where their son's precocious talents for drawing found him employment at the age of seventeen as the chief cartoonist for the *London Evening News*. Scouting had been John Hargrave's passion since he had joined the movement at the age of twelve, taking as a scouting name 'White Fox'. Rising rapidly through the scout hierarchy (helped by the publication in 1913 of *Lonecraft*, a manual of outdoormanship for scouts who preferred to camp alone), Hargrave had, by 1919, assumed the position of heir apparent to the movement's leader, Robert Baden-Powell.

As for most young men of his generation, the First World War was a shocking intrusion into his life. A Quaker, and therefore a pacifist, Hargrave joined the Royal Army Medical Corps where he was assigned to the Dardanelles and witnessed the catastrophic military disasters of Gallipoli and Suvla Bay. Profoundly disturbed by the experience, Hargrave's by now virulent anti-militarism was poured into his next book, *The Great War Brings it Home*, a diatribe against war and the corrupted world that had produced it. The book proposed all-embracing world reform and the creation of a non-nationalist society run by an elite of healthy youth, schooled in woodcraft so as to be in touch with the vital life forces of the earth, and practising yoga as a tool for mental discipline. Such views brought Hargrave into conflict with the patriotically orthodox Baden-Powell and soon after the formation of the Kibbo Kift, Hargrave was formally expelled from the Scouts. Baden-Powell's

later verdict on his one-time heir was that he was 'a clever young fellow in a way, good at writing and sketching but eccentric, swollen headed and communistic.'[10]

The new group grew slowly, limited as membership was to those who could accept Hargrave's charismatic but autocratic leadership. The original membership of around two hundred consisted of fellow dissident scouts and a few like-minded left-wing youth groups. By 1923 further recruits had increased the membership to around five hundred, but thereafter schisms and splits took their toll. For those who did remain, the organisation offered the intense embrace of a cult. 'It took up practically the whole of my time, all one's spare time, other than having to earn my living of course,' recalled the photographer Angus McBean who joined the Kindred in 1926 and remained a member until 1932 under the name 'Angus Og' (fig. 80).[11] At the time, McBean was working as a clerk in Liberty's department store in Regent Street. Most of the members came from middle-class occupations and held down weekday jobs, typically as teachers. Hargrave too had to make a living, in his case at a London advertising agency where he worked from the early 1920s as copywriter and layout draughtsman. By that time he had a young family to support. His wife, Ruth Clarke, 'Minobi', was the leader of the Merrie Campers, a group of female woodcraft enthusiasts who had affiliated themselves to the Kindred.

What did the Kindred of the Kibbo Kift do? The core activity in the early twenties was developing their own mental, spiritual and physical fitness through hiking and camping. Weekend camps for small groups or 'tribes' were supplemented by larger gatherings for the whole movement held four times a year. 'Althing' at Whitsuntide was a kind of annual general meeting; 'Gleemote' was held in the Autumn; there was a Kin Feast in winter and an Easter hike in the spring. Children were welcomed on all these occasions as the Kindred placed great importance on the development of healthy outdoor habits in the next generation.[12] Between times the Kin kept in touch through their newsletters, *The Mark* and *The Nomad*, both of which were largely platforms for Hargrave's ever more intricate ideas about his, and the Kibbo Kift's, mission.

Ritual and costume were essential elements for the group. Hargrave despised conventional clothes for being the grey uniform of industrial slavery: a 'bowler hat is comic. It is pathetic – a tragicomedy –

81
Kin members outside their tent, 1928
Photographed at the Second Dexter Fam camp

82–3
Ceremonial
tabard, c.1925
Appliquéd felt, front
and reverse, 100 x
72 cm. Worn by 'Will
Scarlet' in his role as
Kin Herald

the headgear of purposeless routine.'[13] For Kibbo Kift activities members donned special costumes more appropriate to the movement's beliefs and ostensibly more practical for outdoor life. For ordinary hiking, the men wore a specially designed outfit 'suitable for the journeyman-craftsman, the pilgrim and the camper,' which mainly consisted of shorts, jerkin and cowl of green, grey or brown. The women's equivalent was a one-piece dress to the knee, leather belt and headdress – with 'something of the Valkyrie in its helmet-like design'. The 'exercise costume' was based on Hargrave's beloved Red Indians, with loincloths for the men and short skirts for the women. Exercise and physical games were always part of camp activities, as was the cultivation of a splendid body. Hargrave, as always, set the standard himself and his fit and athletic body was much admired.

The third form of costume was the outfits worn by the Kindred's office bearers for ceremonial occasions, but never when outsiders were present. These consisted of highly coloured surcoats or tabards, each appropriate to the wearer's role and

displaying a badge symbolising their function (figs 82–3). The organisational structure into which the office bearers fitted was a tight pyramid. The elected Head Man, always Hargrave or 'White Fox', was in charge of general policy. Beneath him was the Deputy Head Man, in charge of organisation and a Kin council made up of six elected officers: Chief Scribe, Chief Tally Keeper, Chief Ritesmaster, Chief Campswarden, Chief Gleemaster, Chief Redesman, plus Head Men of districts. In 1922 the movement only ran to two districts: Watlingthing, whose Head Man was Green Flame, and Wandlething, whose Head Man was Eagle, but others were created later. Although the movement was firmly co-educational, women were not eligible for office, and even the movement's most devoted member, Kathleen Milnes or 'Blue Falcon' (fig. 84), who was responsible for creating the great illuminated manuscript Kinlog (fig. 85), only did so 'acting under a mandate issued by the Chief Scribe', 'Batwing'.

The ceremonials were elaborate affairs devised by Hargrave to include naming ceremonies, rites and quasi-mystical chants. At the great gatherings, the opening ritual consisted of the Saying of the Peace of the Kin by the Reader; the Sealing of the Lips by the Chief Ritesmaster; the Bidding and the Bode by the Deputy Head Man; Wending Away by the Head Man. Ceremonials and chants were written down and put in the care of the Chief Ritesmaster, but there were also some unwritten ceremonies which Hargrave conducted in a 'Taboo Tent' to which only select members were admitted. It was doubtless this Taboo Tent that gave rise to accusations of occult practices. Hargrave's fondness for esoteric turns of phrase did not help his denials, but he always insisted that the Kibbo Kift had no need of dark forces: 'This is no mystical cult, occult clique, nor magical fraternity. Nor is it a secret nor semi-secret society. The Great Secret is open to all. That which is living does not look for life. A wan spiritualisation manifest in a thousand and one "spiritisms" makes a mockery of mankind. Arise, break through, stand upright!'[14]

Back in the workday world, Hargrave began a career as a novelist as a way of supplementing his income from the advertising agency. *Harbottle*, published in April 1924, was something of a bestseller, going into four editions in eight months. It is a workmanlike comedy of modern manners in which a bluff Northern manufacturer on a business trip to London falls for the charms of a flimsily-dressed flapper. She seduces him into buying her a West End flat and then, in a typically 1920s treatment of the 'New Woman', proves to be thoroughly immoral by blackmailing him. Chastened by his lesson in life, he buys her off and returns to the loving arms of his virtuous wife. Hargrave's next novel, *Young Winkle* (1925) was considerably less well received. Most critics had no quarrel with the basic story but

complained, to Hargrave's fury, that long pages of economic analysis had no place in a novel. These interruptions reflected Hargrave's latest obsession.

If the Scout movement and the Great War had been the two initial influences on Hargrave, the economic theories of C.H. Douglas were the third. Hargrave encountered them in 1923 after his employer introduced him to Douglas, a maverick economist whose radical theories, expounded in a series of books published from 1919, challenged every economic assumption of the day. Douglas

84
Kathleen Milnes, 1928
'Blue Falcon' was photographed at the Gleemote in 1928 in her ceremonial costume and holding the Scaldic staff.

The Kinlog, 1927
Kathleen M. Milnes (d.1943), 55 x 40 cm. This page records the start of the Kindred's belief in Social Credit, here represented by scales with consumption and production in equal balance.

argued that in order to avoid another world war, economies had to be totally reconstructed so as to allow consumption to keep pace with production. The fault in Douglas' view lay in 'the cost-accountancy system used throughout the civilised world.' He proposed instead a redistributive system of 'Social Credit' whereby a 'just price' adjustment on each commodity would close the gap between an individual's purchasing power and retail prices, thus bringing consumption and production into an equal balance (fig. 85). Every individual would receive a share of the 'National Dividend', which would provide for all, including those who chose

not to work, thus ensuring a more equitable balance between individuals, fair shares for all and automatic social harmony.

The theory had a profound effect on Hargrave to whom it gave a real focus for the movement's hitherto rather vague notions of world peace and harmony. The key to a better future was now not just the development of super-fit individuals but also a specific economic programme. The Kindred would not just be a woodcraft tribe but also a political cell. Not all the Kibbo Kift shared his views. In 1924 a group associated with the South London Co-operative movement departed to form a separate organisation, The Woodcraft Folk, which espoused more conventional socialist beliefs. As Hargrave himself admitted, social credit 'split the movement from top to bottom because a good many Kinsfolk wanted to get on with their camping and handicrafts, and they hoped world peace would come about by hoping.'

By the time Hargrave wrote *The Confession of the Kibbo Kift* in 1927, Utopian economics were central to the Kibbo Kift mix and his political views had moved far beyond parliamentary democracy. Democracy was a reactionary movement which held back progress by being weighed down by the apathy and inertia of the mass. Not only that, it legitimised itself by reference to 'the average man', a concept the fiercely individualistic Hargrave found offensive: democracy was a sham, 'a ritual dance-mask . . . carved in the likeness of the average man.'[15] The political model for the Kibbo Kift was the small cell of highly disciplined elite 'culture carriers' who would effect change by, in Hargrave's words, 'penetrating' or 'fertilising' the chaotic flux of the many: 'The Kindred looks upon itself as a Positive Upright Fertilising Principle, and the creative

climax of *Lingam in Yoni* is reached when it has penetrated Inertia and given form to formlessness.'[16] He saw similarities all over the world where small closed groups were 'swaying the emotions of the Great Mass' – Sinn Fein, the Bolsheviks and the Italian fascists. In all cases he considered these groups profoundly misguided for ignoring the bigger picture of world economics that Social Credit revealed. But he saw in them the proof that 'the Active Few always influence the multitude.'

The Confession of the Kibbo Kift was the first public statement of the aims and mission of the Kibbo Kift. Its mix of ideas is eclectic to the point of bewilderment, yet overall it conveys an unmistakable 1920s energy and a 1920s method in its apparent madness. The Kibbo Kift was all for nature, Taosim, Indian yoga, Norse myth and animism; some of the ideas behind Bolshevism, fascism and Sinn Fein; pacifism and non-violence; the automation of machinery, Red Indian woodcraft, spiritual and psycho-sexual energy, Tolstoy, physical fitness, upright posture, creative play, Druids, sitting in silence, 'the flexible fluid undertow' of the unconscious, primary colours, disciplined behaviour. The Kibbo Kift opposed: war, patriotism, democracy, Bolshevism, fascism, all political parties including Sinn Fein, the 'Charlie Chaplin civilisation', 'the syncopated civilisation', slouching, giggling, George Bernard Shaw, homosexuality, the 'New Woman', Nesta Webster (who was one of their critics), mass suggestion through propaganda and advertising, mass media, mass housing, work in general (a cause of unemployment), and above all international finance. The degree of 'Englishness' in this eclectic mix will be discussed in the third section of this chapter.

Symbols

The dance, the lilt, the great chant, the rousing song, the deep music, take shape unconsciously from the true beat of the heart in silence, just as all the graphic and plastic arts can only recover vitality and meaning from a body-sense of the Sphere, the Pyramid and the Cube.

John Hargrave, 1927[17]

Hargrave's considerable artistic and literary talents were as strong an influence on the Kibbo Kift as his ideas. As always, he placed his own interests at the centre of the group's activity, but justified this with a substructure of theory about what function they fulfilled. Art, or 'creative play' as it was called when children were involved, was certainly not about art for art's sake, but was more about communication, fulfilling the Kinsman's obligation 'to keep himself alert and able to express ideas fearlessly and effectively.' Hargrave's idea of fearless and effective communication was idiosyncratic. Although recognising words were 'idea-carriers', he constantly railed against their deployment in the service of logic and reason: 'we feel ourselves cut off from one another, wrapped about in tight fitting words and almost strangulated by cleverly devised systems of ideas.'[18] Words were often 'word worms', nasty things that ate into the soul. Visual symbols, on the other hand, left room for the soul to breathe.

From the beginning Kinsfolk were encouraged to be creative by decorating their tents and rucksacks, keeping illustrated diaries, making their own clothes and carving their own totem poles or crests, based on their Kin names (figs 80, 90 and 93). Around 1926 this sort of activity increased when one of the members, C.W. Paul-Jones, 'Old Mole', was given the

86–9
Designs for sigils, 1928
John Hargrave (1894–1982), diameter 20 cm. The symbols were worn by Kinsfolk mandated for special work: *(from left)* Kin writer, Kin photographer, Tom Tom Chief and Transport Chief.

**90–93
Ceremonial
carvings, 1925–9**
(from left) White Fox
totem, height 46 cm;
The Great Crest,
an important
ceremonial item,
height 59 cm; Head
of the Scaldic Staff,
carried by Kinsfolk
when reciting sagas
at gatherings, height
43 cm; Dove totem,
height 27 cm

job of encouraging the others, not a difficult task
since many Kinsfolk had been attracted to the
movement for its interest in things artistic and the
group included several art students and teachers. The
performing arts were also encouraged: hiking songs
were written and published in Kibbo Kift song
books, and mumming plays were written and
produced, all with elaborate costumes and stage sets,
often designed by Hargrave. Some of the
movement's most appealing surviving artefacts are
the archery equipment made for the Company of
Archers, formed in 1928 under 'Eagle' (Reginald
Dixon, an internationally famous archer) and his
wife 'Dione' (figs 94–5).

Although art was a collective Kibbo Kift activity,
the movement's central imagery remained in the
care of the Head Man. It was he who designed the
ceremonial outfits, regalia, symbols and 'picture
writing' which held the movement together.
Hargrave's interest in the use of signs and symbols
was evident through his many books on Red Indian
woodcraft: *Lonecraft* (1913), *Wigwam Papers* (1916),
Totem Talks (1918) and *Tribal Training* (1919). Red
Indians enjoyed something of a revival in children's
literature in the early 1920s and besides seeing
these earlier books republished, Hargrave also
produced the *Boys Book of Signs and Symbols* in 1923.

Hargrave's work in the advertising agency may well
have added another dimension to his interest in
visual communication. He was certainly sufficiently
aware of modern developments in corporate
identity to register the Kibbo Kift as a 'British
Monomark' in 1926.[19]

The 1920s saw several attempts to develop a new
language of communication through symbols rather
than words. The best-known are Otto Neurath's
'isotypes' which were devised in Vienna in the
1920s. Neurath approached the issue as a scientist,
aiming to construct a non-culturally specific
language that could be universally understood: the
signs for man and woman found on the doors of
public toilets across the world are testament to his
success. Less longlasting were the symbols devised
by the Ministry of Transport in the late twenties for
Britain's first road signs, such as the flaming torch,
the symbol for 'school' (fig. 35 shows the more
straightforward sign for crossroads). Hargrave's
sign language has some of both approaches.
Drawing heavily on Red Indian lore, some symbols
were reasonably universal: wavy lines for water,
vertical lines for rain etc. But his interest in
Egyptian hieroglyphics also produced some visually
esoteric devices – the sign for 'worship', for
example, was a strange merger of cross and amulet.

94–5
**94–5
Armguard, 1928**
(above) Design by
Hargrave, 12 x 25 cm;
(below) Archer's
leather armguard
embroidered by
'Dione', 17 x 30 cm

For the Kibbo Kift's 'sigils' or badges of office, Hargrave produced composite abstract devices, whose meaning is usually literal but not always obvious (figs 86–9). The organisation itself was usually represented by a triangle or a phalanx of triangles, derived from the shape of a tent. The Head Man was a stylised face with an all-seeing eye, or sometimes a disembodied mouth. Countryside was a pine tree. Mechanised society was cogwheels and angularity. Nature is usually a group of curvilinear elements such as branches and leaves, sometimes in combination with the upright form of the KK letters which to Hargrave had a very clear meaning of positive strength and virility, bringing Yang to Nature's Yin.

Colours were significant: 'use the three primaries and the three secondaries in their full values and let the atonic crawl away blinded. The vital man uses vital colour – red, yellow, blue and gold. Heraldic, primitive, full-blooded, vigorous. Let them crawl away to their "toneful" half shades.'[20] Black and white were energy and inertia, but any contrasting colours side by side usually signified a kind of Yin Yang meeting of opposites. Shapes were also significant. The circle, triangle and square had mystical connotations but also represented for Hargrave a shorthand for social structures: the circle was tribal society, the pyramid Western social structure, and the square the ideal to be aimed at (the triangular Kindred were only an instrument to bring the square about). 'Social structure says the Kin should be "on the square".' It should be quadrilateral, right-angled and expansive – an elastic-sided cube – within which the individual understands his economic obligations of association but is not pressed upon from the top.'[21]

Hargrave was proud of the movement's visual style: 'Tent decoration, picture writing, and all kinds of primitive Art . . . until now we might also claim to have established a sort of KK style of our own in the designing and decorating of our equipment.'[22] Did this new style produce anything other than art applied to the movement's artefacts? It seems not. As a commercial artist Hargrave was probably predisposed to dislike professional painters and the theorising of the Bloomsburies would certainly have infuriated him. A sense of the irrelevance of much of the contemporary debate about art comes out very clearly in *The Confession*, particularly in Hargrave's exposition of the 'fixed hierarchy of the visual arts in their order of importance.'[23] At the top was the Splendid Body, followed by the art of manners, the art of dress, architecture and finally 'the minor arts of painting and sculpture'. These, he explained, had been relegated to fifth place because they were only the reflections of reality and the first four are expressed in terms of reality and are therefore more important. The irrelevance of the conventional art world also comes out in a passage describing his exasperation at attending a workers education lecture on art appreciation, in the course of which the lecturer complained that the workers lacked colour in their lives. 'If they want colour,' exploded Hargrave, 'give them colour – in their lives. Strip off their degrading trousers and give them slashed

96
Social Credit is Coming, c.1931
C.W. Paul-Jones, gouache on paper, 35 x 25 cm.
Showing the paramilitary uniform of the Kibbo
Kift adopted in 1931. Paul-Jones ('Old Mole'),
one of the movement's most talented artists, left
in 1934, uncomfortable with its new direction.

figure. After *Young Winkle* in 1925 he produced three relatively mainstream novels in the late twenties before the production of his literary masterpiece in 1935. *Summer Time Ends* was a Joycean attempt to capture modern life in an eight-hundred-page-long verbal stream. Among its fans were James Agate, John Steinbeck ('it does seem to be a very great book'), Louis MacNeice, Hesketh Pearson and Ezra Pound ('for an absolute record of the state of the English mind in our time, no volume of recent years has surpassed it').[25] But Cyril Connolly, writing in the *New Statesman*, concluded: 'I found this book literally unreadable.' And the *Observer*'s reviewer A.G. MacDonald was moved to despair: 'there are moments when a conscientious reviewer feels like bursting into tears . . . I must confess that my main feeling about it was that whereas summer might end, this book never would.'

By the time *Summer Time Ends* appeared, the Kibbo Kift had taken on a new life as the Green Shirt Movement of Social Credit. Hargrave had brought the first phase of the Kibbo Kift's existence to a formal end in January 1931 when he announced the restructuring of the organisation as a whole, the arrival of a new group from Coventry – the Legion for the Unemployed, and the adoption of a paramilitary uniform of green shirt and beret (fig. 96). This change, completed in 1932, marked the realisation that the movement needed to become less visibly eccentric in order to make mainstream political headway. With Hargrave still at the helm, the party turned into a more conventional minority political party, similar to the red-shirted communists and black-shirted fascists with whom the green shirts often clashed. Instead of hiking and camping, the group now concentrated on marching and public meetings, all to promote their single cause 'Demand the National Dividend'. A campaign of

scarlet and cloth of gold and heavenly blue, star-emblazoned! Chuck their nasty cloth-caps and bowler hats in the dust-bin and give them the feathered cap and parti-coloured hood. But just standing staring at pictures in the Tate Gallery . . .'[24] As already mentioned, perhaps the nearest parallel among more conventional twenties artists is Eric Gill. Gill, like Hargrave, was a maverick, but also mystically inspired, with a strong reverence for the body as the receptacle of spiritual and physical energy. Gill also saw conventional male clothing as the expression of man's degradation and would have thoroughly applauded Hargrave's call for the workers to be clothed in feathered caps and coloured hoods.

In the literary world, Hargrave's career as a novelist made him a more conventional, albeit still maverick, symbolic civil disobedience materialised, resulting in disturbances in the House of Commons, a green painted brick being thrown at the Bank of England in 1938 and a green arrow shot through the door of 11 Downing Street in 1940. In 1937 the movement, by now several thousand strong thanks to the appeal of social credit to the unemployed, became a casualty of the Public Order Act designed to curb Oswald Mosley's Black Shirts. An attempt to circumvent the ban on paramilitary uniforms by marching with green shirts carried on coat hangers proved futile and the Green Shirts effectively disappeared from English public life. Hargrave briefly reappeared on the political scene in 1950 when he stood for the parliamentary elections in Stoke Newington as the candidate for the Social Credit Party of Great Britain, but he lost his deposit.

Spirit

Does everything happen in London? The Important Thing may yet happen in Lostwithiel or Peper Harow, or Hinton-in-the-Hedges, to be merely reflected in London. You think it is all Dunlop tyres and cheap radio sets? But no, the spirit of the people is not here, not here.

John Hargrave, 1927[26]

So what exactly was the nature of the Kibbo Kift's Englishness? Although the movement's eclectic mix of enthusiasms and influences was *sui generis*, a not inconsiderable patch of common ground existed between them and those of their contemporaries who also saw post-war English society as distressingly barren. In its early days the movement had attracted some more mainstream British thinkers, including the former suffragette Emmeline Pethick Lawrence, psychologist Havelock Ellis,

novelist H.G. Wells, Indian philosopher and poet Rabindranath Tagore and biologist Julian Huxley. Patrick Geddes, the founder of town planning, was a sympathetic fellow traveller, as was D.H. Lawrence who was probably not alone in liking the movement's aims but disliking Hargrave: 'He's ambitious and his ambition isn't practical . . . he's overweening and he's cold. But for all that, on the whole he's right, and I respect him for it. I respect his courage and aloneness. If it weren't for his ambition and his lack of warmth, I'd go and Kibbo Kift along with him.'[27]

Lawrence's interest is not surprising. What he and Hargrave shared in common was the feeling that mankind in its modern rational phase had strayed too far from its primitive roots and somehow needed to reconnect with its darker, more vital nature. Whereas Lawrence saw non-European aboriginal cultures as the gateway to these essential energies, Hargrave found them in the English past, in the semi-mythical worlds of Wayland Smith, Piers Plowman and Beowulf. In looking to the past for inspiration, Hargrave was, of course, subscribing to a well-established view of the English past, one in which industrialisation had brought with it a catastrophic destruction of human values: England before industrialisation had been a green and pleasant land for freeborn Englishmen; afterwards it was a human slave ship where men were chained to machines by the heartless and soulless worship of money. This picture of England's recent past had emerged in its most fiery nineteenth-century form in the writings of John Ruskin, Matthew Arnold and William Morris, all of whose views underpinned in some form virtually the whole spectrum of thinking about the nature of English society in the first half of the twentieth. From Christian Socialists to Conservatives, all seemed agreed that in some

**97–8
Transport banner,
1929**
John Hargrave
(1894–1982),
appliquéd felt, front
and reverse, 60 ×
65 cm. A 'banner
flottante' designed
by Hargrave on the
theme of transport:
on the front, a
modern car, and
on the reverse, a
hooded kinsman
with the upright
K sign

way English values had irrevocably altered for the worse in the preceding century, despite the great benefits of wealth and world prestige that industrialisation had also brought to the country.

It is easy to see Hargrave within this wide spectrum of dissatisfaction at the England he saw around him, and – on the evidence of the quaint costumes and the interest in folklore – to place him probably at the more left-wing end of this spectrum. His Utopianism had some parallels with that of William Morris: his vision of the healthy future was, like that of Morris, fed by aesthetic distaste at the smoke and grime of cities, and a sense that things had been better in the distant past of villages and hedgerows. But Hargrave was always keen to distance himself from 'the pinkos', and placed himself more in sympathy with Conservatives who, he said, were more amenable to discipline: there was nothing he disliked more than 'the unsubdued mind'. This belief in self-discipline imposed from within could perhaps be seen as Hargrave's Quaker values erupting through the pagan trappings of his organisation. It is also a clear signal of the post-war flavour of his vision: the Kibbo Kift's Utopia emerged from an age of mass democracy and an international situation perceived as chaos, a period when the results of indiscipline were all too apparent in every sphere of life. As we shall see in later chapters, discipline was also the quality that was being called for in relation to London's built environment. Hargrave would almost certainly have agreed with Frank Pick, also from a Quaker background, who attributed the visual chaos of London's streets to a lack of discipline. The prescription for improvement, according to Pick, was not so much external controls but internal restraint: 'Discipline is of two kinds. That which results from outward compulsion (and we are too stiff-necked a people to produce any good effect

from that), and that which results from the inward acceptance of an ideal.'[28]

The twenties character of Hargrave's vision also comes through in his attitude to machinery and work. Although neither Ruskin nor Morris were against machinery as such, they still saw machines as part of man's fall from grace and therefore taking only a subservient role in production in the future which would reassert the moral and spiritual value of handicrafts. By Hargrave's time the possibilities of a craft-driven future had long since gone and his vision saw a future in which all work would be undertaken by automatic machinery, thus liberating mankind from the bonds of wage slavery. As one of Hargrave's cartoons proclaimed, the Kindred were 'all for machinery – all against the "Mechanised man".'[29]

Hargrave had nothing but scorn for those who persisted in seeing work as a sacramental activity and who therefore approached the problem of unemployment by talking of 'the criminality of idleness':

There is not the slightest reason, moral or otherwise, why people should not be idle if they wish to be, when automatic machines plus a comparatively few highly skilled and highly paid engineers and mechanics are able and willing to produce essential supplies and a margin of luxuries for general distribution . . . If Mr [George Bernard] Shaw wants, for some reason, to eradicate the terrible vice of idleness, there is but one way of doing it; and that is to see that everyone is idle.[30]

In Hargrave's Utopia, everyone would be paid through the National Dividend and work would become an honour and a privilege for the elite few who proved themselves capable of undertaking it. In answer to the question of what the masses would do with their idleness, Hargrave was optimistic because in his Utopia everyone would be a fully rounded, self-realised individual: 'the Kindred, unafraid to tell the People when they are fools and why, has absolute faith in the ability of the toil-released masses to make good use of their leisure without moral lectures from those who already enjoy it.'[31]

Hargrave's English vision was also twenties in its global scope. The vision was no longer to reassert Englishness in the interests of nationalism or patriotism, but to tap into more universal forces of human energy. Anything that disrupted the free flowing of these forces was to be deplored, whether it was nation states or groups defined by class or race, all of which he rejected as misguided. Even Sinn Fein, whom he admired for springing from a Gaelic cultural movement, had betrayed itself, in his view, by demanding a nation once again: 'a movement of the Sinn Fein type is the attempt of a fly to get out of a spider's web and to become a spider with a web of its own.'[32] The analogy also held for all nationalist movements, movements based on class or religion, political parties and all groupings by race ('sweeping simplification, classification, and characterisation of race – such as the famous Nordic, Mediterranean and Alpine divisions – are abstractions liable to lead to the same deadlock as the Abstract Average Man of Democracy').[33] Partly because of this, Hargrave's opposition to the network of international finance was resolutely not anti-Semitic: 'for centuries the Jews have been a convenient scapegoat. But in fact the social-economic troubles of this country and the world today have nothing to do with any particular race. The present economic-financial system could not be run satisfactorily by a Company of Angels and Archangels from heaven.'[34]

What exactly Hargrave's concept of Englishness was, if not based on racial or national identity, is not altogether clear. But the key to it was clearly within the individual: The Kindred 'wants England to be England, just as it wants Mr Smith to be Mr Smith and not simply "a British national". It holds up no external enemy, but points within. It says "You are Mr Smith – be Mr Smith! For England and the World."'[35] The key was also in vaguely defined 'regions' rather than nations (echoing Patrick Geddes' belief in regional geographies as the basis for planning), thus the Kibbo Kift's Englishness was a localised and 'regional' expression of something more universal 'the common past of the whole human race.' In other countries, according to Hargrave, the movement's natural growth would root itself in the language and culture of other regions, but all these movements

Trained themselves—
For the fight
Made ready;
Still seeking
The key
To the riddle
Of these days.

99
The Kinlog, 1927
Kathleen M. Milnes (d.1943), 55 x 40 cm.
The central image is taken from a cartoon
by John Hargrave and shows the Kibbo Kift
emerging from 'the dreamflod of the unconscious'
flanked by its spiritual mentors.

Germany, which were to develop in more sinister directions in the 1930s. But despite Hargrave's grand universalist theorising, the movement remained rooted in its home country, not just in its fondness for a mythical English past, but also in its fierce individualism and its belief in the forces of energy and spirituality that flowed through the individual and through place. The Kibbo Kift also remained rooted in its time in its total rejection of the old world, whose economic, political and spiritual muddle was deemed to be beyond salvation; and in its conviction that change was only possible through the Yang qualities of strength, energy and self-discipline.

A similar combination of quasi-mystical beliefs and a disciplined approach to life was not uncommon in 1920s England. Such tendencies were certainly found in the writings of Patrick Abercrombie, the town planner whose 1926 book, *The Preservation of Rural England*, the founding document of the Council for the Protection of Rural England, invoked the Chinese practice of Feng Shui.[37] Abercrombie wished to 'order' things appropriately, but to do so while respecting and harmonising with the invisible forces at work in particular places. The craft and mystery of the planner was to provide a holistic, spiritually harmonic environment, not merely a dryly rational allocation of functions. Underneath the extremes of Hargrave's vision, there is something of this same, perhaps typically English, approach to national progress: the belief that chaos on its own was destructive, that order must be brought, that the individual and the spirit must be respected, and that these matters were better handled by a priesthood of self-disciplined experts who would address themselves to individuals, rather than politicians who addressed themselves to the mass.

would have the same regenerative mission 'because the basic economic problem throughout the world is the same for all' and the spiritual channels would all be in tune. 'Along these lines will develop that Universitas of flesh and blood which, because of its common force, uniformity and obligation (rooted in the regional past of each locality), will give a change of direction to the world-flood from left to right, releasing personality within the Invisible House of the Holy Body of Man.'[36]

The Kibbo Kift did have contacts with similar groups in other countries: with hindsight, the most significant of these were the youth groups in

Chapter 6

London

London is bound to be indifferent. It is part of the bigness and substantiality of this metropolis, as it is the law of this orderly universe, upon which most of our individual freedom depends. And there is no freedom for the individual like that which is bestowed upon him by the indifference of London.

Alfred Noyes, 1926[1]

How did the ferment of ideas and events outlined in the previous chapters have their effect on London as a physical city? Did London's buildings and streets only function as an urban backdrop to the comings and goings of views and opinions, or did the city itself respond to the new insights into what made the world go round? London certainly saw substantial physical changes during the decade. 'Perhaps in no seven-year period has the face of London changed so much as it has done since Armistice Day 1918,' observed Sir Lawrence Weaver in 1926.[2] To Thomas Burke, writing in the early 1930s, the changes he had witnessed in London over the past forty years were so radical and far-reaching that no other period in London's history could possibly match them in scope or scale. As an optimist, Burke thought these changes were decidedly for the better. Compared to the 1890s, London was now a cleaner, lighter place; there had been an easing and brightening; the city felt less solid and complacent, more rejuvenated and vigorous.

The catalysts for change in the physical aspects of twenties London were, of course, more than ideological. To Burke, 'the chief material agents, acting under our very noses, were undoubtedly petrol and electricity.'[3] He might also have added concrete, tarmac, steel-framed buildings, and

wireless and telephone technology. However, it was thoughts and ideas about London's present and future that activated these material agents of change, and these ideas were many and various. Some, like those touched on in previous chapters, were imported from overseas: from America, for example, came the notion of 'zoning' as a basis for town planning. But of all the strands of thought about London during the decade, two were perhaps fundamental, both of which were homegrown and both of which had surfaced and resurfaced in discussions about the city for many years previously.

On the one hand there was the notion that London needed somehow to be made to work for the good of all its citizens, that there was a public good London had visibly to embody over and above the private interests of individuals or companies. On the other was the question of the degree to which London needed to be constrained, controlled and tidied up. London had always been an unplanned and untidy place, but calls for the city to be forcibly beautified, calls which had been gathering strength since the late nineteenth century, were countered in the twenties by those who pointed out that this very untidiness marked London out as the capital of a freedom-loving race:

100
***Winter*, 1928**
C.R.W. Nevinson
(1889–1946),
tempera on board,
78 x 52 cm.
Nevinson presents
London in winter
mood as a solid,
working city
dominated by
the presence of
dockside industry.

London is like the English character: it is the stronghold of individualism in architecture as in all else. If it be compared with the Paris that Baron Haussmann created, or even with New York, Berlin or Madrid, it is a city without form. The orderliness, co-operation and acceptance of aesthetic authority, which makes an effective art of town planning, appeal to the logical mind. But we have a contempt for logic in architecture as in public affairs: we will not be regulated or regimented.[4]

The last three chapters of this book look at matters which illuminate both these themes: how a twentieth-century London emerged during the 1920s as a city with a renewed sense of the public interest embodied in its public spaces, streets, buildings and services; but also as a city in continual debate as to how controls could be reconciled with the city's traditional virtues as a place of diversity and individual freedom.

Public

Victoria's death was not the end of the nineteenth century, nor was Edward's. The true end of that century, and the beginning of the twentieth and of new-age growing-pains, was the end of the Great War. Not until 1920 did London enter upon its new era of structural and spiritual change.
Thomas Burke, 1934[5]

The main civic task for London, according to some observers, was to make this city of the jazz age harmonious and beautiful. London was no longer to 'typify the clashing of interests and the irresolution of masses. Our duty to posterity is to weld these together and make London a harmonious whole.'[6] The idea that London could be transformed into an 'ideal city' or 'city beautiful' was not exactly new, but what characterised the twenties chapter of the debate was the fervour with which the vision of the ideal city was linked to the public sphere. The public sphere was now generally acknowledged to be one of the most important criteria by which London as a city would be judged as civilised. Public efficiency and public beauty were the twin virtues that the modern civilised London must demonstrate.

This enthusiasm for the public good was encouraged by several things. Democracy had brought a new impetus to improving the living conditions of the urban masses. Petrol and electricity had made brighter, cleaner streets more practically possible than they had ever seemed before. The war had brought visible proof that the city could function collectively. As is certainly well documented for the Second World War, the experience of being a city in a war zone acted as a social leveller. All Londoners, whatever their backgrounds, submitted to rationing, food queues and the restrictions enforced by the Defence of the Realm Acts; all felt the fear of zeppelin raids, and 'men developed a habit of talking fraternally with strangers.'[7] London also acquired a new visual harmony, at least at night, thanks to the policy of painting streetlamps blue – an effort to make London invisible from the air. The resulting blue glow cast a strange beauty over the city: 'one had the feeling that London had been embalmed and bestowed in a mummy-case . . . Brilliant searchlights probed and wiped the sky; we of the streets lived in a blue mist and seemed to breathe blue mist.'[8]

If a cleaner, brighter London seemed within the bounds of possibility, the tools for bringing

101
Victoria Embankment, c.1924
C.R.W. Nevinson (1889–1946), oil on canvas, 48 x 60 cm. A view from the window of the Savoy Hotel, capturing some of London's landmarks and eyesores

change about were also more evident. As the state had extended its interest in the private lives of individuals through old age pension and unemployment insurance, so other legislative 'intrusions' into private life, including property rights, no longer seemed quite so controversial. It was not thought unreasonable for the new Ministry of Health, for example, to seek to control building development in the interests of public health, nor for the new Ministry of Transport to decide what major roads should be built where, regardless of who owned the plots of land. New lines were being drawn about what individuals could and could not do in the interests of the public good, and this quickened the pulse of those who saw in twenties London the possibility of an ideal city.

This is not to say, of course, that drawing new lines between individual rights and the state's demands was never controversial. 'The theory that a man may do what he likes with his own is universal, but in England it is supreme,' said an editorial in the London Society's journal, going on to suggest that 'although the inside of a man's house is his own, the outside is not, as the public has a right to prevent him from defacing the streets with bizarre elevations or hopelessly bad "ornaments".'[9] This suggestion, along with a parallel suggestion that redundant city churches should be turned over for secular public uses such

102
London's cross-river traffic, 1926
G.H. Davis, *The Illustrated London News*, 18 December. Illustration of the scheme put forward by the Royal Commission on London's Cross-River Traffic for an 'artistic double-decker bridge' at Charing Cross

as libraries and art galleries, was promptly denounced by a writer in the *Architect* as unacceptably 'Bolshevist in character'. Controversies also raged over who was to assume the role of custodian of the public good, particularly where public services were concerned. Were public services to be provided by companies wholly operating through democratic government, or by semi-private, semi-public companies enabled to operate in the public interest by being given a monopoly in their field?

A good illustration of the tenor of the twenties debates about the public good is the discussion surrounding London's railway system.[10] For many, London's railways symbolised everything that the London of the future should avoid. The system was a classic nineteenth-century product of profit-driven competition which had resulted in a completely illogical and inefficient network as each individual railway company had built their own terminuses served by their own lines. This competitive hotchpotch had left central London without a central station and, to add insult to injury, the railway companies had also torn London to shreds and brought ugliness to the city by pushing their lines and bridges through traditional street patterns. A source of particular venom was Hungerford Bridge which was continually heaped with abuse as 'an object of shame', 'an active and passive eyesore' and 'the

ugliest structure in Europe' (fig. 101).[11] Railways were also blamed for encouraging London to spread into the countryside in an uncoordinated way, and for de-beautifying the city through the smoke and soot that steam trains expressed continuously day and night, blackening London's buildings and destroying Londoners' lungs.

No-one, of course, wanted to banish rail transport completely. But the vision of London in the future for many twenties commentators was of a city served by a unified railway system under some co-ordinating authority, run for the public good and the beautification of the city. London of the future would demolish its surplus stations and pull down its ugly bridges. It would neatly separate long distance and suburban traffic, take passenger luggage on underground railways to where it needed to be. It would erect stately new stone bridges to enhance the river view, over which would proceed clean smokeless electric trains into a magnificent new Central Station, the envy of Europe and to which passengers from all parts of Europe would flock admiringly through the wonderful new Channel Tunnel, then confidently expected to be built within the next decade (fig. 102). London of the future would be a co-ordinated, orderly London, exuding efficiency and beauty, and designed to serve the greater good of the public, rather than the narrow interests of profit-driven companies.

**103
Memory studies,
1924**
Vera Wheeler
(fl. 1920s), water-
colour, 29 x 39 cm.
From a series of
three sketchbooks
kept by Wheeler
during her time as an
art student in London
in the mid-1920s

People

*Occasionally in Cardiff I saw some Lascars . . . and
sometimes a Greek or an Italian name over a
battered store, but that was all. London changed all
that. It is a capital, and a port, and big at that; so
it is cosmopolitan. I had never seen anything like it,
and I still think the parade of peoples and colours
and tongues just about the best thing in London.*
Glyn Roberts, 1933[12]

Who were the public to whose good the city
was now to be dedicated? Who were the
Londoners filling the smoky trains that clattered
over Hungerford Bridge? Was it really true that,
as Thomas Burke said, 'where ever you go, you
find that the "typical London crowd" is composed
mainly of people who were born far from
London'?[13] Partial answers to all of these
questions can be obtained from the statistical
overviews that planners and politicians of the
time used to deduce what the public wanted and
needed. Statistics erupted wherever state action
coincided with daily life, and as government

developed more tentacles, so new data-sets about
Londoners appeared.

Every year the London County Council published
a thick volume of *London Statistics* which by the
1920s covered many aspects of life and death in the
capital. From the 1925 volume alone we can see
that the estimated population of Greater London
was 7.7 million, an increase on the 7.4 million
recorded at the 1921 census.[14] The most populous
borough was Wandsworth which, at 340,900
people, had just overtaken Islington's 339,000. The
borough with the highest proportion of women
to men was Paddington, but South Kensington was
the only parliamentary constituency where, in the
October 1924 election, women voters outnumbered
men. St Pancras North had the highest electoral
turnout in that election when 79.3% of the 38,041
people eligible to vote did so. In Islington, 6706
babies had been born in 1924, but Shoreditch had
the highest birth rate compared to the size of its
population. Out of the total of 85,147 babies born
in inner London in 1924, 3497, or 4.1%, were
illegitimate. There were 505 suicides in 1924 and
the biggest cause of death was heart disease, which

claimed 7735 Londoners. Three men and two women were tried for murder that year, none of whom received custodial sentences; the guilty were 'otherwise disposed of' which, according to a footnote to the statistical table, meant put to death. 37,393 Londoners were prosecuted for offences against the Road Traffic Acts involving motorcars, and an additional 2890 for offences involving bicycles. 42,769 Londoners borrowed books from Wandsworth Library and 268,454 visited the London Museum in Kensington Palace.

The 1921 census had established a way of classifying people by occupation, instead of purely by industry, and according to those returns, twenties London remained, as it had been throughout its history, a city numerically dominated by manual workers. For many, the main divisions in society continued to be those of social class and London continued to reflect these divisions through place: the upper class being associated with the centre (fig. 104), the middle class with the suburbs (fig. 105) and the working class with the East End (fig. 106), a geographical situation which, with its concentration of the unskilled and the unemployed, was seen as making them peculiarly vulnerable to poverty. It was concerns about the working class and the supposed 'threat' to the skilled and semi-skilled posed by high birth rates among the unskilled, that fuelled calls for birth control and led to the first British birth control clinic being opened in 1921 in the Holloway Road by Marie Stopes. Stopes was one of the promoters of birth control who saw its benefits primarily in terms of social management, although she also recognised its effects on individuals, particularly women.

Divisions of race and ethnicity were not recorded as such in official statistics. Places of birth were recorded by the census, but this did not pick up Londoners from cultural backgrounds other than

104–5
Regent Street, 1926
Putney Hill – Sunday Morning, 1926
Frederick C. Dixon (fl. 1920s), etchings, 42 x 37 cm, 38 x 43 cm. Dixon, a student at the Royal College of Art from 1924, offers a rather unsympathetic view of West End street life and a glance at suburban Londoners busy with their weekend amusements.

106
The Prince of Wales, 1927
Photographed visiting Windsor House in
Wenlock Road, Shoreditch, a Corporation of
London housing development, on 18 October

English, for example Clerkenwell's well-established Italian community. The ten-year gap between the censuses also makes it hard to pin down London's short-term but influential population of students from Empire countries. However, even without official statistics there seems no doubt that the overseas communities, although not numerically as large as they are today, were very far from hidden in terms of the image and character of London. To writers, artists and visitors in the twenties, one of London's essential characteristics continued to be its parade of people and tongues: 'London is not English any more than New York is American – both are international.'[15]

As with social class, certain districts were associated with certain communities. Besides Clerkenwell's Italians, Limehouse in East London was London's Chinatown, becoming doubly famous in the twenties thanks to the success of the Hollywood film, *Broken Blossoms*.[16] In this 1919 tearjerker from a story by Thomas Burke, Lillian Gish played a dockworker's daughter who falls in love with a poor but noble-minded Chinaman and is consequently killed by her abusive father. Burke's sympathies in the original novel were entirely with the Chinese, and this was carried over faithfully into the film which painted a lurid contrast between the civilised and thoughtful 'yellow man' and the brutal and bestial Cockney. By the 1930s, it was said that American sightseers would sometimes take a taxi to Limehouse to see for themselves London's Chinese underworld.

The most cosmopolitan district in London was, of course, far nearer the centre. At the heart of the city, 'a population composed of representatives of half the nations of Europe, and even some of South America makes the labyrinth between Oxford Street and Leicester Square a quaint exotic oasis in the drab wilderness of London.'[17] Soho's traditional European character had come from its

French and Italian communities, but its cosmopolitan tendencies were strengthened in the twentieth century first by war, and then by the nightclub craze that came afterwards. War had brought large numbers of European refugees, alongside the French, Belgian, Italian and Serbian soldiers who used London as a place for home-leave along with the American, Canadian, Australian and African troops.

By the twenties, Soho also housed a floating population from all countries of the world, attracted by the louche feel of the place, cheap lodgings and increasing opportunities for work in the new night-clubs and bars. Black musicians in particular found work in West End clubs, such as Rectors on the Tottenham Court Road, run by the American owner of the Hammersmith Palais. Dan Kildare, the Jamaican pianist who led the band at Ciro's nightclub until his suicide in 1921, was one such performer.[18] London's cosmopolitan mix was a prominent aspect of the twenties city centre and grew stronger as the West End's new 'democratic' entertainment venues brought even greater social and cultural diversity onto the streets. The East End's Jewish young made Leicester Square's Corner House restaurant, theatres and cinemas their own. 'I imagined when I first saw them,' said Glyn Roberts, 'that these people, so magnificently colourful and glossy and self-assured, must be very important and wealthy indeed – the women were so luxurious and the men so blasé. But I found out that they were really very poor; that they invaded the West End in their tens of thousands only twice a week or so; that they spent next to nothing.'[19]

Away from the West End, the presence of black and ethnic Londoners was less visible en masse but often remarked upon, usually in terms that underlined their exoticism:

107
Chinese restaurant, 1920
S. Begg, *The Illustrated London News*, 10 January. This view shows a 'typical Eating House in the Chinese Quarter of the East End' where the fare included 'Fried Noodle, Sharks' Fins, Sea Slugs, and Savouries of Bamboo Shoots'.

London . . . offers more than one nesting place to her outland birds; of whom the well feathered commercial and professional elements prefer, if Latins, the semi-detached respectability of Bayswater and Holland Park, and if Teutonic or mid-European, the *banlieues* of Brondesbury or Highgate; while Asiatics impart a *bouquet d'Orient* to Wimbledon or perch within earshot of the Muezzin at Woking.[20]

Individuals and families from all parts of the Empire were scattered across the city.[21] Pockets of Indian and African students were living in Paddington, where Dr John Alcindor, 'the black doctor of Paddington', was one of the borough's four Medical Officers of Health. Black and Asian men confined to low status jobs tended to congregate in areas of cheap lodgings, notably the East End and Bloomsbury. There were black Londoners living in Acton, Bow, Battersea and in Regent's Park Road where No. 17 was leased by John C. Payne, choirmaster of the Southern Syncopated Orchestra, and was said to have become a meeting place for black artists, writers and musicians.[22] No. 22 in the same street was the home of Eddie Manning, one of London's notorious twenties gangsters. Dr Harold Moody lived in Peckham and spent the 1920s as Director of the

Colonial Missionary Society, a position from which he gathered much food for thought about the development of the black race, all of which informed his foundation in 1931 of the League of Coloured Peoples.

That London was, in John Cournos' words, an 'amazingly international' place is really not so surprising considering that it was not just a city at the heart of the Empire, but also the world's largest port. Goods and people from overseas flowed naturally and easily in and out of London (fig. 108). However, the twenties saw legislative checks to this free trade in people, notably through the Aliens Order of 1920 which made clear legal distinctions between British citizens and 'aliens'. The order was essentially a response to the refugee crisis that affected Europe in the aftermath of the First World War: in 1926 it was estimated that Europe had 9.5 million refugees, of which at least 2 million were Russians displaced by the revolution. All European countries fell back on nationality as a way of controlling the movement of people, and in Britain the climate produced the first appearance of the British 'blue passport', which, it was said, even the Foreign Secretary now had to carry. Citizens of the British Empire were not officially considered to be 'aliens', but those citizens who also happened to be coloured were sometimes caught up in the new attitude of

LONDON'S TRAMWAYS

CALEDONIAN MARKET
EVERY FRIDAY
CALEDONIAN ROAD AND CAMDEN
ROAD TRAMWAY SERVICES

**108
London's
Tramways
poster, 1923**
G.G. Patterson,
152 x 101 cm.
Designed for the
London County
Council, the poster
portrays a market
trader surrounded,
Britannia-like,
by second-hand
goods from around
the world.

suspicion to those who were obviously 'other'. The Special Restriction (Coloured Alien Seaman) Order of 1925 magnified the potential for injustice, and many African, Indian and West Indian seamen found themselves arbitrarily registered as aliens, irrespective of whether they had passports or certificates of British nationality. In the same way, the 'race riots' of 1919 in the port towns of Liverpool and Cardiff were ostensibly against 'aliens' but in practice saw mob violence directed at indigenous black communities. In London, 1919 saw several instances of violence against Black and Aisian seamen in the East End.[23]

As the twenties progressed, fears about 'aliens' were compounded by fears about unemployment, and several bodies across the political spectrum came out as 'Little Englanders'. In July 1920 the London County Council banned foreigners from all council jobs. By the middle of the decade, the Musician's Union had begun its hard-line campaign for a ban on the American musicians, largely black, who were filling the positions in West End club bands and hotel orchestras. To Thomas Burke, such restrictions on skilled people who happened to have been born abroad did nobody any good. Why not a ban on provincials as well? 'If a musician who speaks Italian is barred from England because English musicians are out of work, why should a musician who speaks Yorkshire be allowed to work in London when London musicians are out of work?'[24] He suggested an immigration fee of a hundred guineas for all provincials who wanted to come to London and further deterrence in the form of 'plates of poisoned tripe at the northern railway termini and poisoned pasties at the southern.'

The increasing exertion of official control over the movement of people did affect individuals, as the MP Shapurji Saklatvala found out in 1927. The government banned him from entering Egypt and his passport endorsement permitting him to travel to India was cancelled, effectively barring him from the country of his birth for the rest of his life: following protests his passport was eventually issued and he did manage to make his visit. What was still many years in the future was the idea that the state should exert controls over other aspects of individual's lives in the interests of the public good. In 1930, a Dr A.M. Shah complained to the Home Office that the Streatham Locarno, a dance-hall, had refused him admission on the grounds that he was an Indian.[25] The letter of reply from a Home Office official informed him that there was no remedy at law, which indeed there was not at the time since behaviour which did not result in criminal injury was entirely a matter for the individual. In the same Home Office file is a complaint from an unnamed MP who had taken his guest, 'a distinguished Indian', to a pub near Seven Dials only to be refused service on the grounds that that particular establishment had not served a coloured man for the last ten years. 'This is not a matter, I think,' replied the official, 'on which the Home Office can interfere.' London would have to wait forty more years for the idea that the public good demanded not just beautiful buildings and efficient services, but also fair treatment for all citizens.

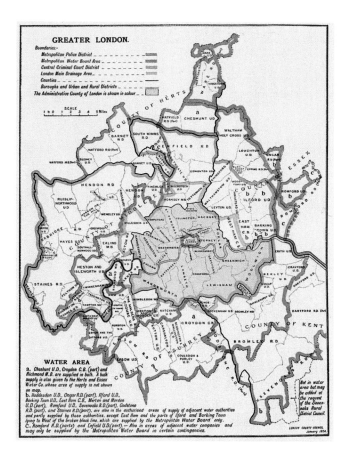

Government

The citizen of Glasgow or Manchester knows the boundary of his city. As he walks through its streets he knows that every public service which is there in evidence is under the control of the Council which is elected by him and his fellow-citizens: the streets, the pavements, their maintenance and cleansing; the production and distribution of gas, electricity and water, the schools, the trams and omnibuses, the police who direct the traffic, public baths, libraries, hospitals, ambulances, museums, recreation grounds, market sewers, public conveniences and a host of other things. How different, however, all this is in London, where everything is divided.

A. Emil Davies, 1925[26]

Population was not the only aspect of London characterised by diversity. By the 1920s, London's public services were provided by a uniquely complex, overlapping network of around a hundred and fifty public authorities, private companies, quasi-public bodies and voluntary charities. Besides the one London County Council (LCC), which had authority for some aspects of inner London, Greater London as a whole was subject to government by twenty-eight metropolitan boroughs, five county councils, three county borough councils, sixty-three urban district councils and eleven rural district councils plus the City of London. There were forty-four Boards of Guardians, forty-one Distress Committees, a Metropolitan Water Board, a Pensions Committee, one overarching Port of London Authority, which incorporated other smaller boards, and two London and Home Counties Joint Committees to co-ordinate traffic and electricity, the provision of which was largely

in the hands of private companies. National government had control over the Metropolitan Police Force. To add to the confusion, the areas which each of the various 'London' authorities covered had different boundaries (fig. 109). And of course many services run for the benefit of the London public operated outside the London government network, notably London's great hospitals, all of which relied for part of their income on charitable appeals (fig. 110).

The complexity of London's government reflected London's massive size and the pragmatic way the public sector had been extended over the past eighty years, which tended to be through inventing new bodies to deal with new matters. The presence of private companies in London's public services, such as the suppliers of water, gas, electricity and transport, also reflected how attractive London's large population had always been to business: a large population promised equally large profits. By the 1920s London did have a single democratically elected body in the shape of the LCC, which in theory could form the focus of any attempt to

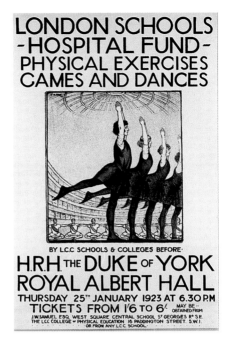

**LONDON SCHOOLS
- HOSPITAL FUND -
PHYSICAL EXERCISES
GAMES AND DANCES**

BY L.C.C SCHOOLS & COLLEGES BEFORE·

**H.R.H. THE DUKE OF YORK
ROYAL ALBERT HALL**
THURSDAY 25TH JANUARY 1923 AT 6.30 P.M.
TICKETS FROM 1/6 TO 6/ MAY BE OBTAINED FROM
J.W.SAMUEL ESQ. WEST SQUARE CENTRAL SCHOOL ST GEORGES R° S.E.
THE LCC COLLEGE OF PHYSICAL EDUCATION 16 PADDINGTON STREET. S.W.1.
OR FROM ANY L.C.C. SCHOOL·

**110
London Schools
Hospital Fund
poster, 1923**
F.M. Grey, 76 x 50 cm.
Designed to publicise
a fundraising event
for the Hospitals of
London Combined
Appeal

simplify this patchwork. However, the strategic role which had been envisaged for the council when it was created in 1889 was, in many people's views, compromised by its small size. The LCC's authority only extended to inner London, 'the administrative county of London', and not the whole of Greater London which had to be taken into account for virtually any strategic matter. 'One of the most pressing problems in connection with the development of London,' said the town planner Raymond Unwin, voicing a very commonly felt view, 'is the creation of some unity of control, with a general staff to think out and plan the policy for this great city.'[27] But this ideal seemed very far from London's reality.

Perhaps not surprisingly, voices from within the LCC led the calls for the patchwork to be rationalised under a single governing body. In 1920 the young and energetic London Labour Party, under the leadership of the young and ambitious Herbert Morrison, announced its campaign for a Parliament for London – 'Home Rule for London' – with its vision of a greatly enlarged county council covering the whole of Greater London: controlling the transport and electricity, absorbing the Water Board, the Asylums Board, the police and the Port of London Authority, masterminding a comprehensive development plan for Greater London and inaugurating new public services for the public good. 'We hold that the

primary necessities of life must gradually be removed from the realm of private profit to that of public service, with the emphasis upon the word "service".'[28] This comment almost certainly referred to transport and electricity, the two privately run public services that caused the London Labour Party particular apoplexy and where the 'municipal socialism' practised in England's provincial cities was the model to which they enviously looked: 'Birmingham and Liverpool would no more dream of allowing their gas and electricity to be under private ownership, and would no more play into the hands of an international traffic combine, than they would think of allowing their drainage system to be operated for the profit of a foreign country.'[29]

Morrison's vision was not universally inspiring, and among the most unenthusiastic were, perhaps surprisingly, those of his colleagues in the London Labour Party who were active in London's thirty-two borough councils. To the boroughs, the LCC was already unbearably overweening and municipal socialism, if it was to come, would be far better implemented at the local borough level. The clash between county and borough came to its most famous head in 1921 when the Labour-controlled borough council in Poplar refused to levy the LCC rates for police and asylum contributions which had been fixed at a uniform rate for the whole county and thus failed to take account of local differences, such as the high unemployment among Poplar's rate payers. The councillors were accordingly imprisoned, but 'Poplarism' had made the point that governing London without taking into account local differences was fraught with political pitfalls.

Morrison's vision of Home Rule for London was also not shared by all the members of the LCC. Since 1907, the council had been under the control of the 'Municipal Reform' party who tended to be the party

111–12
London's Tramways posters, 1926–7
152 x 101 cm.
The London County Council used designs both from students at the Central School of Arts and Crafts such as Edward Walters, a wood engraver *(left)*, and professional firms such as Ralph & Brown Studios *(right)*.

of the status quo: 'every attempt to impose fresh duties on the council, to extend existing services, or to initiate anything for the community, is to be resisted for the primary duty of the council is to spend as little of the rate payers' money as possible.'[30] The Labour opposition's view of the Municipal Reformers was somewhat caricatured. But the Municipal Reform majority definitely did not agree with Morrison's calls for Home Rule for London, and neither did the 1921 Royal Commission on London Government which came down against the idea of a Greater London Authority and in favour of further specialist strategic bodies, such as a London and Home Counties Traffic Authority, which came into existence soon afterwards.

The twenties did see vigorous LCC bursts of activity, despite the Municipal Reformers' professed reluctance to spend money. By far the largest service run by the council was London's education system, which provided unity in at least one area: the new education scheme 'takes us a long step towards the provision of one organised system of education for London.'[31] By the mid 1920s, the LCC was running most of London's educational institutions, from elementary schools to vocational technical institutes. It was also providing school meals, nursery schools, scholarships and teacher training institutes. Education was the largest heading in the council's expenditure, amounting, by 1924–5, to £12 million out of a total council expenditure of almost £26 million.

The tramways, for years a controversial council responsibility which some thought should be returned to private ownership, were run as a 'revenue-producing service' and promoted to the public as never before through posters, some designed by students at the Central School of Arts and Crafts (fig. 111).[32] By the twenties, London's tramway system constituted the largest municipal network in the world, and despite suffering from the increasing competition of motorbuses, continued to be essential in London's central area, providing cheap, albeit spartan, public transport. New tram cars were introduced and many tramway posters from the late twenties emphasised that trams could be comfortable and quick, as well as cheap and reliable (fig. 112). Cynics suggested that this new investment in the tram service was merely a way of making trams more attractive to Lord Ashfield's powerful transport consortium which already ran the tubes and buses and which had set its sights on becoming a monopoly.

Another active area for both LCC and borough councils during the twenties was housing. The catalyst for this activity was the State Assisted Schemes set out by central government in the Housing Acts of 1919, 1923 and 1924, all of which offered such generous subsidy arrangements for house-building that even the most parsimonious Municipal Reformer could not turn the offer down. The 1919 act also allowed local councils to raise money directly from the public by issuing bonds (figs 113–15). This 'interesting development in county council finance'[33] also generated an interesting development in 'peacetime propaganda', as the LCC set up a central publicity committee for a campaign to sell housing bonds in London not just on behalf of its own programmes, but also in support of metropolitan borough initiatives (fig. 114). The first campaign for 6% bonds

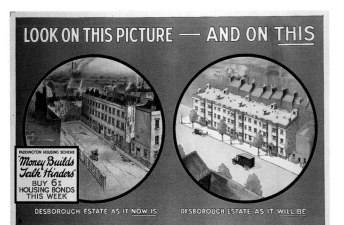

took place between April and September 1920 and resulted in just under £4 million being raised, proof, it was said, of Londoners' civic spirit. The housing undertaken by the metropolitan boroughs consisted of small blocks of flats within borough boundaries. Bethnal Green, a small but active borough, had constructed four hundred flats by 1925, all lit with electricity – the modern fuel of the future, and some also using electricity for cooking and heating. Bethnal Green's housing programme achieved national notoriety in July 1927 when the Bolshevik-minded housing committee announced that their newly built rehousing sheme at Parminter Street was to be named the Lenin Estate. After much to-ing and fro-ing, the name 'Cambridge Heath Estate' was adopted instead.

The LCC also built flats on inner-city sites, largely as part of slum clearance programmes. But most of its housing effort was focused on the green-field 'cottage estates' on the outskirts of London. Transplanting Londoners from the disorderly surroundings of the inner city to the fresh air of the suburban countryside was a policy that had been begun before the war. Post-war, the LCC's major scheme was the mammoth Becontree Estate at Dagenham to the east of London (see appendix). Dwarfing in size all of its predecessors, it was conceived in 1919 as 'the creation of a new township, complete in itself, a task of greater magnitude than had ever been attempted in the history of housing.'[34] This estate, a typically twenties massive-scale solution to social problems, was indeed a new town, taking up a 3000-acre site laid out for 26,000 houses to rehouse 130,000 people, a population equivalent to a town the size of Brighton and largely aimed at skilled workmen's families from Bethnal Green and other overcrowded East London boroughs. The estate took many years to build: by December 1927, thirty-eight miles of road had been laid,

113–15
London 6% Housing Bonds posters, 1920–21
76 × 51 cm, 101 × 151 cm, 152 × 101 cm. The propaganda campaign for housing bonds was directed by Edward S. Shrapnell Smith and appealed on several fronts. The bottom poster shows County Hall, the London County Council's lavish new head-quarters, under construction.

116
Laggard Leaves,
1925
Harry Bush
(1883–1957), oil on
canvas, 36 x 26 cm.
The artist's back
garden at Queensland
Avenue in Merton,
a typical suburban
development of
densely laid out
terraced houses.
Bush exhibited at
the Royal Academy
from 1925, invariably
taking suburbia as
his subject.

140 million bricks had been used and eighty miles of sewers installed. But ten years after the start, the estate remained incomplete with none of the churches, community halls, sports grounds or doctors surgeries originally envisaged. There were no pubs and public transport was limited, which meant long journeys for workers such as Bill Waghorn who moved to Becontree in 1929 but kept his job on the Isle of Dogs:

> In those days you couldn't be late to work, what with three million unemployed and no work available anywhere, so I ended up by cycling the fourteen-mile round trip to and from work. I had to get up at five o'clock every morning every day and I didn't finish work until nine o'clock at night, so it was quite an ordeal.[35]

The arrival of the mammoth Ford factory at Dagenham in 1931 was a godsend for Bill Waghorn.

Becontree is a good example of the strengths and weaknesses of those who governed twenties London with the idea of public good in mind. To politicians, the general public was a homogeneous, statistically analysable mass whose needs and wants could be rationally deduced. In the context of the twenties, where public needs largely concerned life's basic amenities, this was not inappropriate: it was a fair deduction that people living in slums would prefer better housing. A mammoth project like Becontree was an enormous credit to local government of the day in the heroic way it tackled the housing problem supposedly once and for all. There is no doubt that it did make a difference to individual lives, and the personal memories of those who moved to the new cottage estates is overwhelmingly that their quality of life improved as a result.[36]

However, treating the public as one homogeneous mass also carried disadvantages. Becontree and its fellow estates were praised in the twenties for their spacious layouts, which were seen as more generous and healthy than the suburban estates produced by private house-builders (fig. 116). Yet even as early as the 1930s, it was the council estates, rather than the private estates, which were being criticised for their monotony, soullessness and industrial qualities.

Chapter 7

City

I might add that I think London, though charming, a most illogical city. I don't know its boundaries: you don't; nobody does.

Stephen Leacock, 1922[1]

The Becontree estate represented not just a new scale of ambition for London's public housing, but also new goals for the city as a whole. Becontree, at least in theory, was an urban environment of order and harmony, where every public need had been anticipated and planned for and where selfish self-interest was held in check by benevolent controls designed to hold the balance between individual freedom and the public good. Over the centuries London had often been characterised as a monster, a terrifyingly uncontrollable organism, voraciously devouring the countryside around it. In the 1920s, a less intimidating metaphor started to appear: London as a tree that 'can be trained and pruned and made to grow this way or that.'[2] This way of thinking about the city gave it a more manageable aspect. No longer 'a phenomenon of nature to be accepted and submitted to,' London was 'a work of man to be guided and controlled.'[3]

The debate about the ways in which London could be guided and controlled into a more orderly direction centred around two aspects of London's development. Firstly, the city's growth into the surrounding countryside at an ever more alarming rate. The monstrous metaphor for London did not entirely disappear during the twenties and it resurfaced memorably in a 1928 book by Clough Williams-Ellis which characterised London as an octopus, its sooty tentacles reaching out into the

117
London's Tramways poster, 1926
Leslie Porter, 152 x 101 cm. Designed for the London County Council to advertise its suburban tram services

whole of the south-east.[4] In the battle to contain the octopus, twenties London deployed an armoury of techniques associated with the newly emerging profession of town planning: enforceable controls on building, zoning, designation of areas 'protected' against development, experts to adjudicate what was or was not in the public interest. These were also the tools to be applied to the second area of disquiet about London's disorderliness, the streets

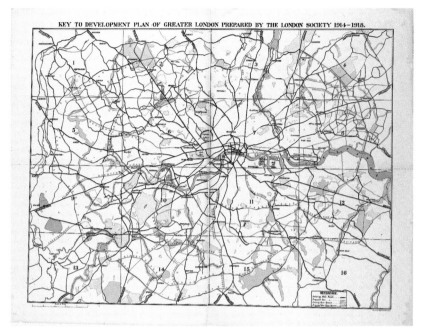

KEY TO DEVELOPMENT PLAN OF GREATER LONDON PREPARED BY THE LONDON SOCIETY 1914–1918.

118
Greater London's roads, 1918
69 x 91 cm. The overall map for the London's Society's Development Plan marking existing roads (in black) with proposed roads (in red). Existing and proposed open spaces are shaded in pale green and darker green. The map incorporates the concept of an inner circular road around London, plus an outer ring, here called the 'Zone Road'.

and buildings at the heart of the city. Cries for a more orderly West End were made on several grounds throughout the decade: aesthetic – as modern buildings got taller and less inclined to fit harmoniously with their older neighbours; practical – a response to increasing traffic congestion; and ideological – the belief that the city should represent public virtues of rational and logical thought. 'The appearance of London is the material presentment of the imperfectly civilised mind of London,' muttered one voice from on high in 1919 calling not just for town planning techniques, but also for a measure of self-discipline on the part of architects, builders, property speculators, shop owners, bus company owners and motorcar owners, all of whom were variously accused of being agents of disorder.[5]

This chapter looks at the changes that fuelled debate about London's disorderly character at its edges and at its centre. Of the two, the second is discussed in more detail and it is arguably the changes at London's centre that was the twenties' most lasting legacy in terms of the built environment. Lawrence Weaver's comment that the seven years between 1918 and 1926 saw a transformation of London's public face has already been noted; Harold Clunn, writing in the early 1930s, asserted that since 1910 London had witnessed 'the greatest amount of rebuilding that has ever taken place

within so short a period of time since the Great Fire of London.'[6] It was during the 1920s that the main shopping streets of central London took on the character they still largely present today. It was also during the twenties that London, arguably, reconciled itself to its own intrinsic disorderliness. Despite a continuous chorus of disapproval against buildings 'miscellaneous and divergent in style' that spoke of nothing more than the 'the showy tastelessness and chaotic imaginations of modern architects,'[7] London emerged from the decade with distinctly more rather than less architectural disunity.

Planning

If logically carried out the plan will add greatly to the happiness of the people of London, for it will provide for a practicable workable scheme with a vision of a city conceived in understanding of the needs of many people, their homes and those matters most connected with their daily life. In it lies the possibility of a city beautiful, one in which ugliness is unnecessary.

The London Society, 1927[8]

'A first essential to the security of a measure of orderliness in the building of a city,' according to the London Society in 1927, was a plan. A plan approached the future of cities with clear-headed rational thought, deciding in advance what was to be built where, and what land was best left to nature. The London Society had been formed in 1912 with the aim of 'the practical improvement and artistic development of London by the united efforts of its citizens.' In 1918 the Society published a large sixteen-sheet map of London which can claim to be London's first development plan in that it marked the main arterial roads, both existing and projected, with the aim of providing a blueprint for future industrial and housing developments on London's periphery (fig. 118).⁹ Although the map had no legal status, it did anticipate some of the major roads built by the Ministry of Transport in the early twenties, of which the most significant was the Great West Road, opened in 1925 and providing, as the London Society had intended, a piece of infrastructure around which industry could settle in a planned and orderly way.

The 1918 map also anticipated the enforcement of a 'green girdle' or legally protected belt of open land around London's edge. This idea had been talked about since the late nineteenth century, but by the 1920s its need seemed ever more urgent. The first official body to consider an overall plan for the whole London region was the Greater London Regional Planning Committee appointed in 1927 by Neville Chamberlain, then Minister of Health. It included the planner Raymond Unwin, one of the green belt's most vocal supporters, and the Committee's first report in 1929 produced a radical vision not just of a green belt but of restrictions on virtually all building on London's outer boundaries. Too controversial for the time, the report was shelved, although the green belt idea finally emerged in legislation in 1938.

The London Society's 1918 map reflected the principles enshrined in the two pieces of town planning legislation that existed on the statute books prior to 1918, both of which confined controls on building development to non-built-up areas. Town planning as it initially emerged in Britain was as much about preserving the countryside as developing the town. Throughout the 1920s calls for controls to be extended to built-up areas grew ever stronger, and, accordingly, the London

Society started work on a large map of central London and a series of 'user maps' showing the occupations and land use in various boroughs (fig. 119). Sometimes these maps were produced by architects employed by the Society, others were a community effort executed by local residents under the Society's guidance ('the Society will provide full instruction together with the maps and even the coloured pencils so as to ensure a uniform result throughout the whole district').¹⁰

By the 1920s the extension of planning controls to built-up areas was already common practice in European and American cities through such concepts as zoning. Zoning, as the London Society explained to its members in 1922, was 'the practice of

119
Southwark, 1928
82 x 69 cm. The base map has been hand-coloured by members of the London Society to highlight their planning ideas. Main and secondary traffic routes are red and yellow respectively: cul-de-sacs are blue. Streets coloured purple are those to be closed off to through-traffic. Other significant points for the Society are schools (orange) and green spaces (green).

120
**All Souls Church
and Upper Regent
Street, 1924**
Ian Strang
(1880–1959), pencil,
23 x 33 cm.
The steel-framed
building dwarfs its
early 19th-century
neighbours. The
east side of Upper
Regent Street
had been entirely
rebuilt by 1930.

dividing a town into a number of districts and then prescribing for each district certain restrictions upon the user and height of new buildings as well as the proportion of site to be occupied by them . . . The object of zones is to control the character and extent of a city's growth.'[11] Zoning had been pioneered in New York in 1916 but remained novel in England, although controls on individual buildings were a less unfamiliar concept in London thanks to the various London Building Acts and London County Council by-laws which provided a measure of control against the erection of dangerous or unhealthy structures. The existing legislation was consolidated in 1930 when the new London Building Act set a new height limit of eighty feet, beneath which buildings could be erected without the need for planning consent: crucially, the eighty-foot limit excluded 'ornamental towers or turrets', a loophole which several architects were to exploit in the 1930s.

In their enthusiasm for controls over the built environment, the London Society proceeded under the optimistic assumption that such controls would be relatively easy to frame since there would be automatic agreement, among men of a scientific frame of mind, as to what controls would best serve the public interest. As the 1920s unfolded, however, debates over buildings, bridges and streets all demonstrated how vast were the fields for disagreement. The most controversial issue was undoubtedly bridges. Even before the war the tangle

of inter-related problems surrounding London's bridges was becoming impossibly intricate: there were not enough road bridges for the current levels of motor traffic; Waterloo, the main road bridge, was too narrow and developing alarming signs of structural collapse; the rail bridges were ugly; river transport interests demanded fewer not more bridges. The Corporation of London rebuilt Southwark Bridge in 1921 and in 1929 began to rebuild Lambeth Bridge, but both were thought to be in 'the wrong place' for relieving the traffic on Waterloo Bridge. For many, the solution was a new road bridge at Charing Cross, but others advanced the cause of a new bridge at St Paul's or at Ludgate. A Royal Commission on London's Cross-River Traffic in 1926 recommended new bridges at Charing Cross (fig. 102) and Ludgate, but in the same year the London County Council voted to demolish Waterloo Bridge – to howls of protests from those who thought it London's most beautiful bridge. It was no wonder that Londoners observing the 'futile wranglings of architects, railway companies and civic corporations over the question of the bridges' should have con-cluded that planning was bringing more rather than less disorder to the city.[12]

Buildings

*I earnestly hope that we shall never contemplate
putting up 'sky scrapers' in London.*

Dean Inge, 1921[13]

Harmonising the shape and style of individual buildings in London's centre was as ambitious a task as restraining London's expansion at its edges. But here the debate was as much about the responsibilities of individuals as the need for

enforceable regulations. Should architects continue to design within the classical tradition, thus ensuring some sort of visual continuity in London's buildings, or should they feel free to respond to the modern age in a more adventurous way? That the decade allowed adventurousness was admitted by all. New construction methods based on steel frames and concrete were making new shapes and scales of buildings possible. Architectural debate was moving away from 'the academic point of view which identifies the idea of architecture entirely with classical and Renaissance forms and insists upon them as a fixed and unalterable standard.'[14]

Perhaps the most critical factor was the changing needs of commercial clients, most of whom demanded buildings that were big. Retailers needed mammoth department stores with large expanses of plate glass window at street level; property developers dreamed up giant blocks of flats in London's centre; banks and firms required new head offices as amalgamations and mergers pushed virtually every sector in the economy through a 'corporatising' phase. Two of the largest giant corporations to emerge from the decade were Imperial Chemical Industries (ICI), formed in 1926, and the Midland Bank, which became the biggest bank in the British Empire on its amalgamation with the London Joint Stock Bank in 1918. As discussed below, the Midland's new head office in Poultry was typical of the scale and style of these twenties corporate palaces, stretching the classical vocabulary to new heights, and adding a distinctive late-imperial bulk to the City of London's streets.

Ian Strang's drawing of a steel-framed building under construction in Upper Regent Street in June 1924 (fig. 120) illustrates the new scale of building that spread through central London throughout the twenties as leases fell in and four-storey nineteenth-century buildings were replaced by six- or eight-storey ones.[15] Height records started to creep upwards. Adelaide House begun in 1921 was London's tallest commercial building at forty-five metres until the construction of the fifty-three-metre high Broadway House in 1927. The 'Oxo Tower' on Stamford Wharf begun in 1928 topped sixty-one metres to become London's token skyscraper, although the empty structure was more in the nature of a very tall clock tower (see appendix). Similarly empty was the elaborate sixty-seven-metre high tower on top of Triton Court in Finsbury Square in the City, designed in 1929. Debate about the desirable height of London's buildings ran throughout the decade, fuelled by the many picture features in the press on the extraordinary skyscraper landscapes of American

121
The Co-Optimists,
1925
Norman Howard,
The Graphic, 19
September. 'One of the most thrilling sights in London at the moment, the men who are at work on the new buildings being erected on the site of Devonshire House'

**122
Design for the
Devonshire House
site, c.1923**
An outlandish
proposal by Edmund
Frazer Tomlins
(1885–1946)

cities.[16] The anti-skyscraper lobby argued on all fronts: the loss of open spaces, darker streets, London's unstable clay soil, traffic congestion and above all the damage to London's character. Even Harvey Corbett, the American architect of Bush House, thought that London was not suited to high-rise because the city's 'quaint old-fashioned atmosphere' should not be transformed into something 'as commonplace and commercial as any of our own American cities.'[17]

Steel framing not only enabled buildings to stretch upwards, but also to join in the fancy dress spirit of the decade. Virtually any sort of decorative façade could be hung from steel girders, from faience tiles to thin panels of bronze or plate glass. Even when a building was faced with stone or brick, to give the illusion of traditional construction methods, the steel frame enabled the exterior to make a decorative statement on its own, uninhibited by the need to hold the building up. A good example was India House, erected in record time (another characteristic of steel-framed buildings) between 1928 and July 1930 as the new

home of the Indian High Commission. India House (see appendix) was designed by Sir Herbert Baker to combine imperial grandeur with a very obvious Indian flavour, underlining the political symbolism of the building as 'a visible symbol of India's advancement towards the goal of Dominion status.'[18] The new building was, it was emphasised in the brochure for the opening ceremony, entirely planned from India as an Indian government project. As one comment of the time also described it, India House was an example of 'scenic architecture' with ornament designed to 'express and impress the Indian mind' overlaid onto a twentieth-century office building: 'it is as if one building had swallowed another whole and yet has shown no signs of digestion in the process.'[19]

Other steel-framed buildings dressed themselves to suit. Roman magnificence and Egyptian exoticism were favourite styles for department stores and cinemas; domestic Georgian and quaint Tudor appeared on blocks of flats; the grocers Fortnum & Mason's also chose Georgian but with rococo flourishes; the Carreras cigarette factory in Hampstead was modelled on an Egyptian temple and Atkinson's perfumery in Bond Street was turned into a medieval fairy palace (see appendix). The traditional classical vocabulary of architecture did not disappear entirely but became at times just another decorative style to be hung on a steel frame for effect, infuriating architectural purists: 'Oxford Street is incongruously punctuated by massive dry goods stores, pretentiously camouflaged as sham Greek temples . . . Overdecorated façades with a massive futility of pillars upholding nothing and based apparently on a fragile foundation of plate-glass and lingerie make Bond Street ridiculous.'[20]

The blame for this outbreak of individuality in architecture was, perhaps inevitably, laid at the door

123
Proposal for the Devonshire House site, 1923
C.F.A. Voysey (1857–1941), watercolour, 27 x 37 cm. Voysey's scheme showing two of the three thirty-storey residential tower blocks

of America. 'Although the confession sounds like treason,' declared the writer James Laver in a 1924 essay entitled 'Last Week in Babylon', contemporary London 'is somehow less London than it was, its peculiar flavour diluted by hygiene and American architecture.'[21] American architects certainly had a hand in three of twenties London's most significant new buildings: Bush House, the new Devonshire House and Ideal House, all three of which symbolised to some degree the American conquest of London. Bush House, as we have seen, dominated the great Kingsway scheme, London's one pre-war attempt at Parisian grandeur. It also usurped a site that for some years had been earmarked for the British Empire. Before the war Australia House had taken one end of the Aldwych island site and during the war several designs emerged for imperially resonant public squares to be constructed on the plot next door: one such proposed a war memorial honouring overseas troops, designed by Charles Holden and Eric Gill.[22] The imperial vision of the Aldwych was semi-realised in 1930 with the opening of India House at the other end of the

island, but by that time Bush House stood between India and Australia, an uncompromisingly American interloper, deplored by some as a prime example of the modern architectural spirit of vulgar self-assertion and praised by others as a well-shaped American building.

Even more symbolically charged was the new Devonshire House (see appendix), a block of luxury flats on the north side of Piccadilly which was completed in 1926 to designs by Thomas Hastings, a New York architect whose firm's most famous creation to date was the New York Public Library. The building's significance emerged from what it had replaced: the old Devonshire House and grounds, one of the great aristocratic palaces that had stood in Mayfair since the eighteenth century. By the end of the Great War, such visible statements of aristocratic power were both ana-chronistic and uneconomic to maintain, and in 1920 the Ninth Duke of Devonshire moved his household to more modest premises in Mayfair, leaving his large house and grounds in the hands of a property developer.[23] An architectural

124
Ideal House,
1927–9
Architect: S. Gordon
Jeeves (1887–1964)
in association with
Raymond Hood
(1881–1934)

competition in 1923 invited proposals for redeveloping the site, virtually all of which were coloured with some American influence (fig. 122). Most fascinating of all was the proposal by the old Arts and Crafts architect C.F.A.Voysey for three thirty-storey Gothic skyscrapers (fig. 123).[24] Voysey's at first sight extraordinary scheme echoes other views of the time that skycraper living was the logical answer to modern urban problems. 'The only hope I can see for London,' said Sir Martin Conway to the London Society in 1920, 'is to stop building widely, as we do, and build high.'[25] In July 1922 the *Illustrated London News* had reported on the French scheme devised by Auguste Perret, to house 'the surplus population' in 'extra lofty buildings', noting that New York was also looking at this solution to its housing problems.[26] Voysey's own inspiration seemed to stem as much from this practical sense of city planning as any aesthetic delight in high-rise. By providing housing rather than commercial premises, his blocks would reduce traffic congestion in central London, and they were designed for efficient communal living with a

shared dining room on every floor. In the event, the building that finally rose from the old Devonshire site was a vast but smooth, Manhattan-style block of luxury service flats above car showrooms. Although at eight storeys Devonshire House was not a true skyscraper, its construction became one of the new American-style sights of London as workmen went about their business on steel girders high above Piccadilly (fig. 121).

Devonshire House, like Bush House, presented London with American opulence rooted in classical traditions. The third of the American buildings was more uncompromisingly modern. Ideal House in Great Argyll Street (fig. 124) was built in 1927–9 for the American-owned National Radiator Company to the designs of Stanley Gordon Jeeves and his partner William Eve. With a look directly echoing the parent company's building in New York, which had been designed by the skyscraper architect Raymond Hood, Ideal House was an unashamedly flash building with polished black granite surfaces and jazzy coloured enamel decoration. It was an eye-catching and self-assertive block, doubly intrusive to some English eyes in that it stood right across the street to that temple of the Arts and Crafts movement, Liberty's store (fig. 125). The juxtaposition of the two buildings was particularly striking in that four years before the arrival of Ideal House, Liberty's had constructed an extension to their main Regent Street store in an uncompromisingly self-assertive English style.[27] The pastiche Tudor design by E.T. Hall and his son could not have looked more vernacular: the single block conveyed the illusion that this was really a series of small shops; its construction was visibly timber-framed, rather than steel-framed; its decorative details copied Tudor originals. Even architectural critics were a

little taken aback by this Arts and Crafts funda-mentalism, but the London Society thought it an ingenious building which beautified the street. For their Regent Street building, rebuilt a year later in 1925, Liberty's went for stone facings in an imperial and patriotic style, crowning the curved frontage with a massive 35-metre long frieze showing the nations bringing the wealth of the world to Britannia (see appendix). In the neighbouring plot across Great Marlborough Street, Dickens & Jones was rebuilt in 1921 as a modern commercial block hung with bronze panels, large windows and half-Roman, half-Egyptian detailing (see appendix). Perhaps no corner of central London demonstrates more strikingly the architectural diversity of twenties London than the four buildings grouped around the Regent Street end of Great Marlborough Street.

There were perhaps only two districts of twenties London where some sort of architectural consensus held sway. The first was the Grosvenor Estate in Mayfair where development was controlled by the second Duke's estate office.[28] Here the preferred style was neo-Georgian, to match the real Georgian which made up a large proportion of the existing squares and streets. Georgian brick had English and aristocratic credentials and, as a style associated with domestic building, was deemed particularly appropriate for blocks of flats. Several neo-Georgian blocks of red brick with tasteful white stone classical details appeared on the estate in the twenties: Upper Feilde in Park Street is a good example (see appendix). The largest development of all, however, were the great blocks of Grosvenor House on Park Lane which stretched English Georgian to an American scale (see appendix). The consulting architect for this development of flats and luxury hotel, promoted as 'the most modern hotel in

Europe'[29] with such luxurious features as washbasins in every room, was the very English Sir Edwin Lutyens, who had visited America in 1925 and returned reconciled to the aesthetic possibilities of the sky-scraper. The resulting 'cliffs of Park Lane' were not to everybody's taste, not least because of the mismatch between style and scale, as *The Times* noted: 'what is the matter with Grosvenor House is that it is not designed as a big building. It is an overgrown small building, stretching a familiar and endearing style of architecture beyond its capacity to please.'[30] Lutyens' other exercise in designing modern flats occurred at the other end of the social scale but produced, arguably, a more harmonious result. Completed in 1930, the Grosvenor Housing Estate in Pimlico was a rehousing scheme for Westminster City Council and devised by Lutyens as a series of geometric blocks simply decorated with large black and white squares (see appendix). Chequerboard patterns were popular treatments for twenties interiors but only an architect with the confidence of Lutyens would have dared put them on the outside of a building.

The other district of London where consistency of architectural expression was more or less maintained over the decade was the City of London. Here the gravitas bestowed on buildings by classical tradition remained important, and all the prestigious new office blocks of the twenties clung on to a classical or Renaissance vocabulary, albeit while also conveying a more modern sense of mass and scale.

125
Liberty's, 1922–3
Architects: E.T. & E.S. Hall. The department store's 'Tudor House'

127
**Adelaide House,
1921–5**
Architects: Burnet
& Tait

A good example is Britannic House, the new head office of the Anglo-Persian Oil Company, also designed by Lutyens and built from 1921–5 (fig. 126). But the corporate classicism of the twenties was seen most strikingly in the cluster of gigantic new bank offices designed for the streets around the Royal Exchange road junction. As the geographer Iain Black has pointed out, these banking palaces were 'visions of Empire articulated in architectural form,' though the Empire whose glory they proclaimed was as much the new empire of international finance as the old British one.[31] Lutyens' head office for the Midland Bank in Poultry was, like Britannic House, a slightly theatrical interpretation of classical tradition (see appendix). The block next door, designed by Sir Edwin Cooper for the National Provincial Bank at the end of the decade, also took some liberties but remained a statement of solid imperial might. More austerely conventional was the new head office of Lloyds Bank in Cornhill by Sir John Burnet (see appendix) which married classical repertoire to a large scale through a monumental façade of giant columns.

By general consent the least successful of all the massive new arrivals at the heart of the City was the Bank of England itself (see appendix), which began rebuilding on its central site in 1922 in order to concentrate its staff, hitherto dispersed in separate offices. The design by Sir Herbert Baker aimed to please everybody: the Bank, which needed more office space, and the preservationists who demanded that the existing early nineteenth-century structures, designed by Sir John Soane, be retained. The results, which kept Soane's perimeter walls but created within them a kind of wedding cake effect of piled-up classical elements, pleased nobody. A similarly uneasy application of classical and Renaissance styles to a large steel-framed scale was deployed by Sir Frank Baines for the headquarters of the newly

formed Imperial Chemical Industries (ICI) opened on Millbank in 1928 (see appendix). Millbank was twenties London's new office quarter, promoted as an off-shoot of the City thanks to the new link opened up across the south bank by the reconstruction of Southwark Bridge. By 1928 Baines had also begun work on the neighbouring Thames House, an unprecedentedly vast office development trumpeted as the largest office block in Europe. At both ICI and Thames House Baines tried to stretch the classical repertoire across a vast bulk but arguably to weaker effect than that achieved in the City by Lutyens.

Despite the domination of traditional architectural styles in the City, it was there that one of twenties London's most modern-looking buildings appeared at the beginning of the decade. Adelaide House on the north side of London Bridge (fig. 127), was a combined warehouse and office block designed by a British firm Burnet & Tait, whose modern credentials had been established before the war with their 1911 Kodak House on Kingsway. Kodak House had made no secret of its steel-framed construction, and neither did Adelaide House with its strong vertical lines and its large scale. Despite being symmetrical, monumental and faced with stone, the building departed from any sense of classical orders and proportions, displaying instead a fashionable, even jazzy, Chicago-Egyptian decorative style. Adelaide House's expression of the jazzy spirit of the age was also conveyed by the small golf course built on its roof, a novelty much filmed and photographed over the decade.

In its vertical lines Adelaide House echoed another pre-war London building which looked forward rather than back: this was the green-glazed Holland House in the City, built in 1914 to the designs of the Dutch architect J.P. Berlage. Berlage's modern-looking building found another twenties echo in Summit

House in Red Lion Square (fig. 128), designed by Westwood & Emberton as a warehouse for Austin Reed and faced with yellow glazed tiles. Summit House, according to the design authority Lawrence Weaver, was not only of similar type to Berlage's but it was also a 'fresh note of architectural expression' that 'breaks sharply upon the atmosphere of old Red Lion Square like a blast from a trumpet of terracotta.'[32] Perhaps it is no coincidence that freshness in architecture should have been associated with more functional buildings, such as warehouses. If 'modernism' is measured by plainness and elevations expressive of the method of construction, then the most modernist buildings in twenties London were probably warehouses, factories and the many flat-fronted office blocks which mechanistically repeated the formula established by the Kodak Building of stone faced uprights and flat bronze panels in between. It was certainly a small office building which pointed to the shape of things to come at the end of the decade. In 1929 the architect Frederick Etchells, an admirer of Le Corbusier, designed an extension for the advertising agency William Crawford in High Holborn (see appendix). With its horizontal emphasis and puritanically plain façade made from glass and concrete, this building could be said to mark the beginning of a new sort of architectural conformity in London: the hard-line modernist style that was eventually to dominate London's commercial buildings and streets.

128
Summit House,
1925
Architects:
Westwood &
Emberton

Streets

Take our most fashionable shopping street, Bond Street, and in the welter of signs, one blanketing the other, is there either service or beauty? It has become a crazy competition.

Frank Pick, 1923[33]

The twenties view that London's streets were disorderly often went hand in hand with the view that in the past things had been better, that London had once achieved a kind of architectural unity through the regularity and rhythm of Georgian terraces and squares. Ironically, perhaps the nearest the 1920s got to a Georgian-style regular and harmonious street was the new American-flavoured developments around the old Mayfair estates. The new look Berkeley Street, for example, which until the redevelopment had been a narrow street overlooked by the wall of Devonshire House, acquired a unity of architectural expression, thanks to the block-like buildings and grid-like street layout (fig. 130). Streets like this were far preferable, in traditionalists' eyes, to the chaotic nature of the main West End shopping streets, Oxford Street and Bond Street in particular, which distressed those seeking harmony not just because of the assertive

architecture of individual buildings, but also the chaos of competing signage, advertisements, hoardings and unmatching street furniture, not to mention the disorderliness of unregulated motorbuses, private motorcars and untidy crowds.

The increasing chaos of the West End gave a new lease of life to calls for some great Parisian-style imperial boulevards to be bulldozed through the city centre. The long-running debate about bridges included various suggestions for new processional routes: from the proposed new Empire station at Waterloo to Trafalgar Square; from Waterloo to St George's Circus in Southwark; from Trafalgar Square to the British Museum and the new university precinct to be built east of Gower Street. None of these grand street schemes came to pass, although central London underwent an epidemic of street widening throughout the twenties, less on aesthetic grounds than the practical ones of accommodating alarming new levels of motor traffic. Kingsway had been designed to a width of eighty-feet, but even that was not wide enough, according to some:

> Holborn and Oxford Street should be as wide as Whitehall; by a drastic order they should be widened on the south side. They should be increased to a hundred and fifty feet. One trembles at the thought of the cost and inconvenience that would be incurred were such an order insisted on. Yet nothing less will suffice if we are to do justice to posterity.[34]

In the event Oxford Street – like the Strand, Piccadilly and Regent Street – spent much of the 1920s being dug up by workmen, but the repaving only produced a slight widening on its south side.

Calls for traffic controls grew ever louder during the twenties. Ingenious schemes to manage traffic were promoted, such as the concrete flyover across Oxford Circus devised in 1924 by Sir Alfred Yarrow who also offered to foot the bill for the scheme.[35] The first major step in the direction of control was the London Traffic Act of 1924, a crucial piece of legislation which for the first time imposed some controls on the unregulated bus operators who were a large cause of most of the traffic jams in Oxford Street. Henceforth, routes were regulated and certain streets banned for buses. Controls on private cars took a little longer to come, but in March 1926 London's first traffic controls were introduced in the form of a 'gyratory', a one-way traffic system at Hyde Park Corner. This was followed by similar one-way systems in both Trafalgar Square and Piccadilly Circus. In August 1926 London's first traffic lights were installed in Piccadilly Circus. More experiments a year later produced London's first white line road markings when lines were drawn onto the road surface at Trafalgar Square and Oxford Street, together with the words 'Look Left', 'Look Right'. The traffic statistics collected by the London County Council show that the introduction of these controls was long overdue. By the middle of the 1920s Hyde Park Corner (fig. 131) was easily London's busiest road junction with 51,528 motor vehicles and 3360 horse-drawn vehicles passing through per day, as recorded on 14 July 1925. After that came Trafalgar Square with 39,488 motor vehicles, followed by Marble Arch and Piccadilly Circus. In 1925, the only place in London where horse-drawn vehicles outnumbered motor vehicles was, curiously, Tower Bridge.[36]

The increasing presence of private cars in the West End was less a matter of people travelling into the centre than a reflection of the increasing numbers of wealthy people living in the new blocks of luxury flats around Hyde Park and Mayfair. The location of the luxury car trade also underlined the arrival of a

new class of resident. At the turn of the century, London's few motorcar manufacturers and dealers operated in the streets around Long Acre, traditionally the centre of the coach-building trade. The motor trade then gravitated west to Great Portland Street, and by the 1920s was firmly established around Bond Street and the surrounding streets, where all the major international car manufacturers – Fiat, Lanchester, Darracq, Ford, Talbot, Citroën, Austin and Wolsey – had their showrooms. Cars also brought new requirements for garages in central London. In 1923 Citroën built what was claimed to be 'the largest service station in the world' at Brook Green. In 1924 the Bluebird Garage opened in the King's Road, purporting to be the largest in Europe and offering parking space for three hundred cars together with workshops and waiting rooms for

130
In Ever-changing London, 1927
Chesley Bonestell, *The Illustrated London News*, 2 April. Showing the new character of Berkeley Street

131
***In the Rotten Row,
One Evening,** 1928*
Yoshio Markino
(1874–1938), oil on
canvas, 51 x 76 cm.
Exhibited at the
New Studio Gallery
in Knightsbridge in
April 1929 as part
of a series on Hyde
Park at night.

chauffeurs. Other garages were built and imaginative schemes for 'car parks' proposed, among them the Architectural Association's 1925 proposal that Leicester Square be completely reconstructed to form a giant underground garage beneath a garden.

The most important street scheme for 1920s London was unquestionably the rebuilding of Regent Street which finally came to a point of completion in 1927, after almost half a century of dispute.[37] The original Regent Street was a creation of the early nineteenth century. Designed by John Nash, it was both a charmingly picturesque piece of urban theatre and a clever piece of social engineering, creating a new route from the royal quarter of St James to Regent's Park while at the same time marking a new boundary between affluent and poor quarters. The street had been designed as a fashionable shopping street, but by the 1880s many of the shopkeepers had begun to complain that the internal space provided by early nineteenth-century buildings was no longer suitable for modern methods of retail. Since the landlord was the Crown, any rebuilding, even if financed by individual proprietors, had to proceed with national approval.

The rebuilding project turned into a forty-year debate about what London's major street should look like: an imperial way that proclaimed the might of Empire, or a street that served the needs of a nation of shopkeepers, which as far as the Regent Street shop owners were concerned meant large plate glass windows? The long-running debate came to a compromise after the war, and although the settlement was largely in the shopkeepers' favour, the bottom end of the street, the 'Quadrant', was designed by Sir Reginald Blomfield in a more monumental way with a stiff baroque dignity to it (fig. 132). The Oxford Circus end began to be rebuilt in 1920 with virtually the whole of Oxford Circus and Upper Regent Street taller, grander and larger than ever before by 1925. The building design was largely the pre-war work of Henry Tanner whose Roman monumental style set the tone for the two main Oxford Circus stores, Peter Robinson and Jay's. In April 1923 rebuilding started at the bottom end, and by the time this section was completed the rebuilding had remodelled not just the end of the street but also the northwest corner of Piccadilly Circus, which included Swan & Edgar's department store and the

**132
Piccadilly Circus,
c.1930**
Photographer
George Reid (1871–
1933) captures the
divide between the
rebuilt Regent Street
in the shape of
Blomfield's County
Fire Office of 1927
(left) and the older,
messier buildings in
Piccadily Circus.

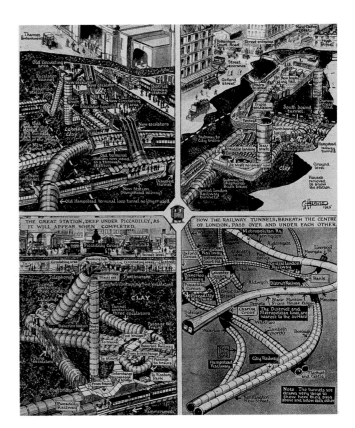

offices of the Sun Fire Insurance Company. Blomfield's stone buildings at the bottom end of Regent Street provided a more austere and dignified effect than the plate glass and bronze at the top, but the gravitas of the scheme was rather undermined by its juxtaposition with the frenetic displays of Piccadilly Circus (fig. 132). Across this irregular space at the heart of London, the new grandeur on the west side faced what was generally agreed to be a disgracefully disorderly mess along the north-east side.

Like the Regent Street rebuilding, the character of Piccadilly Circus had been the subject of much debate over the previous forty years. Still spoken of as 'the heart of Empire', it had also become the world's 'premier publicity site'.[38] Ever since the first illuminated advertisement was erected in the 1890s, battle had ebbed and flowed between the advertisers and those who saw such things as inappropriate eyesores. By-laws allowed the London County Council to have some control over illuminated signs that overhung the pathway, but by the 1920s efforts at enforcing these regulations had petered out. The Crown Estate, who owned the south-west side of the circus, refused to erect signs on their buildings, but the owners of the buildings on the north-east side showed no signs of renouncing their lucrative rental income in the interests of aesthetics. In 1920 a new twenty-one-foot-high illuminated sign was erected, followed in 1923 by two even larger ones, twenty-five feet wide and forty-five feet high. A campaign to tidy up the circus by squaring off its northern side, thus conveniently demolishing all the offending sign-carrying buildings, came to nothing. By the mid-1920s the 'mean and disorderly chaos' at the heart of Empire was a permanent presence.

One of those who thought the north side of Piccadilly Circus unbearably tawdry was Frank Pick, managing director of the Underground Electric

Railways Company, and this perhaps helps explain why the new and magnificent Piccadilly Circus tube station which opened in December 1928 should have so little presence above ground. Pick held that government buildings had little need of self-assertion, but the entrances to the Piccadilly tube station are non-assertive to the point of being almost invisible in the confusion of the circus. The new station had nothing to be humble about. Designed to cope with fifty million passengers a year, it was a triumph of modern engineering, with eleven escalators, an unprecedented number in London's tube system (fig. 133). It was also a triumphant expression of the twenties public service vision with its grand, oval public hall designed by Charles Holden to be lavish yet tasteful, with shop window displays and a world map. It was luxuriously finished in marble and incorporated the latest thinking about efficient design for public spaces.[39] Altogether the new Piccadilly Circus tube station was the model of what a well-ordered city should be: beautiful, efficient and disciplined. Perhaps Pick saw it as a kind of looking-glass counterpart to the Piccadilly Circus above ground, an ideal city beneath the fallible and disorderly one above.

Chapter 8

Systems

There is now no excuse for inaccurate time keeping. The clock which beats the time over the Houses of Parliament ... is heard echoing in the loneliest cottage in the land.

J.C.W. Reith, 1924[1]

In the opening sequence of the documentary film *Under the City* produced by the General Post Office film unit in 1934, the viewer is taken from the skies above London, down through the busy streets to the quiet calm of the subterranean world beneath. These tunnels are 'the arteries' of the city, the network of cables, tunnels and pipes through which the vital commodities of water, electricity and telephone wires travel to where they need to be. The film is a slow-paced production, the camera lingering with Zen-like intensity on details shown in close-up: water trickling, the beauty of texture in the surface of cables, the face of a workman absorbed in his task. There are no lovable Cockney characters in *Under the City*: the workmen and engineers who appear in the film are all skilled men of gravity and expertise. All personify the serious nature of their task: the smooth running of this calm world which allows the great city above to bustle on in all its disordered complexity.

If the great underlying issue of the twenties was subduing the potential for chaos, then London's public services were the area where success could be claimed. By the end of the twenties, London had at least begun to re-order such matters as electricity supply, communications and transport. Indeed by 1929 the results of this new order were already beginning to change daily life in the city in fundamental ways: London's first automatic

telephone exchange had started operation in 1927; in transport the uglier effects of competition had been minimised in preparation for the creation of the London Passenger Transport Board in 1933; a Joint Electricity Authority had begun to assert the public interest in this most crucial modern source of power. Above all, a new sense of mission had started to drive the public sector forward. Making money was no longer enough, the motive was now public efficiency as well as private profit. So highly charged was this sense of mission that some of those caught up in it saw their work as almost spiritual, connected to but not constrained by the mundane, everyday world.

John Reith, then Managing Director of the British Broadcasting Company, expressed something of this spirit in his 1924 manifesto for broadcasting, *Broadcast over Britain*. Just as the world of tunnels beneath the city created its own calm and order, so in the air above broadcasting floated free like spiritual energy, sidestepping all the natural laws of supply and demand that bound more earthly matters such as politics and economics. Broadcasting was 'a reversal of the natural law that the more one takes, the less there is left for others. This obtains in almost all the commonplace happenings of life, but the broadcast is as universal as the air. There is no limit to the amount which may be drawn off.'[2]

Corporations

The phraseology of political controversy continues to reproduce the conventional antitheses of the early nineteenth century; 'private enterprise' and 'public ownership' are contrasted with each other as light with darkness or darkness with light. But in reality, behind the formal shell of the traditional legal system, the elements of a new body of relationships have already been prepared.

R.H. Tawney, 1921[3]

In the down-to-earth world, the debate surrounding the capital's public services in the twenties did indeed largely run along the well worn public/private lines. On the one hand, there were advocates of municipal socialism who insisted that all services, including milk supply, had to be directly controlled by democratic government. On the other hand were those who pointed to the notoriously bureaucratic General Post Office as evidence that the political machine, however democratic, was ill-fitted to operate services commercially. To the Christian socialist R.H. Tawney, the solution lay less in this or that organisational model than in the values and goals that drove companies forward. He called for a 'new condition of efficiency' in which both capitalist and worker rose to the challenge of self-discipline, putting aside their own sectarian interests for the greater good of serving the public professionally.

In actual fact, London by the twenties already had a variety of organisational models for the supply of services, most of which operated somewhere in the middle ground between public and private. The capital's water supply had been the first to move from private to public when in 1902 the undertakings of the eight private water companies and some municipal systems were transferred to a new body, the Metropolitan Water Board. The Port of London Authority established in 1909 also replaced competition between private companies with a unified authority, although in this case the board carried a strong representation from the wharfingers and shipping companies whose interests depended on the port. Transport, gas and electricity in twenties London were all provided by a patchwork of largely private companies, but some measure of co-ordination came with the creation of new advisory bodies: the London and Home Counties Joint Electricity Authority, established in 1920, and the London and Home Counties Traffic Advisory Committee in 1924. Besides water, the main services wholly in public ownership were those operated by the General Post Office, a department of national government with increasingly miscellaneous responsibilities. By the twenties the Post Office operated not only the letter and parcel post, but also the national savings bank, the distribution of old age pensions, wireless licences and the telephone system.

Transport provided a good illustration of the point that efficient public service depended more on values than organisational models. By general agreement, the shining example of a transport company with public values at its heart was the wholly private 'Combine', an American-style holding company that had been formed in 1912 to link the Underground Electric Railways Company of London Ltd, which ran the tube, and the London General Omnibus Company, the largest bus operator in London. Even those ideologically opposed to private ownership conceded that the Combine went about its business in an exemplary public-spirited way, thanks in no small part to the corporate philosophy established by the group's chairman,

134–6
The East Wind,
The North Wind,
The South Wind,
1929
Eric Gill (1882–
1950), Bath stone,
25 x 70 cm.
Three models for
the wind sculptures
at 55 Broadway

137
Bond Street
tube station, 1926
Architect: Charles
Holden (1875–1960).
Photographed in the
1930s

Lord Ashfield, and his managing director, Frank Pick. It was Pick in particular who ensured that the company's ethos of service, responsibility and discipline found expression in the public sphere through the architecture, art and design associated with the company, all of which conveyed to the travelling public a message about the serious and important values that the company upheld.

As a founder member of the Design and Industries Association (DIA), Pick fervently upheld the association's slogan 'fitness for purpose' – the belief that beauty lay in simplicity and usefulness rather than show and ornament. This belief was shared by Pick's favoured architect, Charles Holden, also a DIA member: 'fitness for purpose . . . is more than a slogan, it is a creed; and though it may not be the last word it is most certainly the first.'[4] Holden began work for the Underground group in 1924, remodelling the entrances to some central London stations to make them 'fit for purpose'. At Bond Street, for example, in the heart of the disorderly West End, Holden's ruthlessly bare façade is softened only slightly by detail (fig. 137). Impressed by the results, Pick commissioned Holden to bring the same spirit of public service

modernity to the seven new stations on the Northern line's Morden extension, opened in 1926. Here, Holden's simple yet bulky 'pill box' design brought a standard, almost aggressive austerity to the new stations. Not to everyone's taste at the time, the new stations did nevertheless communicate the corporate identity of the group with its increasingly zealous pursuit of the goal of becoming a public monopoly.

Holden and Pick had a chance to realise their philosophies on a more ambitious scale with the redesign of the Combine's headquarters, 55 Broadway, which opened in 1929 (fig. 138). With its cruciform shape and massive size this building easily attracted the description 'cathedral of modernity'. An uncompromising skyscraper dwarfing everything in its vicinity, the building proclaimed its allegiances to the timeless virtues of modernity, efficiency and fitness for purpose. Needless to say this startling eruption of Pick's underground empire into the streetscape was not without controversy, but debate about the building was nothing compared to debate about the sculptures it carried.[5]

Holden commissioned a number of Britain's modernist sculptors, among them Eric Gill and

Henry Moore, to carve sets of figures representing the four winds (figs 134–6). Set high on the building's upper stories, the wind figures passed above the heads of the public on the ground. However, set prominently above the doors on the ground floor were two specially commissioned works by Jacob Epstein, and it was these two figures, *Night* (fig. 139) and *Day* which attracted a storm of vitriol. The sculptures were seen as making public the 'bestiality that lurks below the surface of our civilisation,' somehow encouraging dangerous primitive urges to come to the surface. *Night* was 'a prehistoric blood-sodden cannibal intoning a horrid ritual over a dead victim.'[6] Both sculptures were vandalised before the storm subsided.

An echo of 55 Broadway, both in the character of the building and the controversy that accompanied its public sculpture, came in 1928 when the design for a new headquarters for the BBC was unveiled.[7] Broadcasting House, designed by George Val Myer, was another cathedral of modernity, a massive white building that seemed to speak of the heavens and timeless values (fig. 140). Like Broadway, it also had its sculptural controversy, this time over Eric Gill's sculpture of Prospero and Ariel, the spirit of the air. In 1930 the matter of Ariel's rather too explicitly modelled nudity was raised in Parliament as an offence against public dignity.

By the end of the twenties the BBC had assumed an importance in national life that few predicted at its beginning when the wireless was little more than a novelty toy. Public radio had begun in November 1922 when the newly formed British Broadcasting Company began regular transmissions from its London Station – named 2LO. Those who wished to receive transmissions paid ten shillings for a broadcast receiving licence and the number of licences

138
55 Broadway,
1927–9
Architect: Charles
Holden (1875–1960)

139
Sir Jacob Epstein
and *Night*, 1929
Jacob Epstein
(1880–1959) was
photographed with
his monumental
creation in the shed
at 55 Broadway in
which he carved his
figure *in situ*.

140
**Broadcasting
House, 1928–32**
Architect: George Val
Myer (1883–1959)

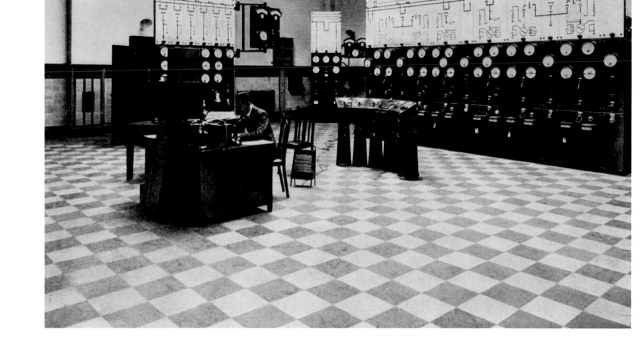

**141
Barking power
station, 1925**
This photograph
shows the power
station's control
room.

issued rose phenomenally from 36,000 at the end
of 1922 to one million in November 1924, two
million in April 1926 and three million by the
end of the decade. The technological foundations
of television broadcasting were also laid in the
twenties with the first experimental transmission
of pictures in 1928. The BBC, like the transport
combine, provided one model for the possible
future organisation of public services. It was a
uniquely free agent, loyal only to its own internal
standards and moral purpose. In 1927 the British
Broadcasting Company was reformed as the
British Broadcasting Corporation, Britain's first
'public corporation' with a constitution that tied
it to no-one. The new organisation was 'vested
with as much freedom as Parliament could be
persuaded to concede' and was run by governors

who were 'deliberately selected by reason of their
personal qualifications and not as representatives
of any specific interests.'[8]

Of all the public services, electricity supply
remained the most earthbound, entangled as it was
in the old arguments of public ownership versus
private enterprise.[9] The crucial importance of
electricity to the development of the capital was
beyond dispute, but the private companies were
particularly well entrenched in their positions,
a point underlined by the fact that the 1919 act
which made the first moves towards nationalising
electricity supply across the country, also allowed
the London electricity companies to protect their
interests legally until 1971. By 1920 a process
of consolidation had produced two dominant
companies: the London Power Company, whose

territory tended to fall in west London, and the County of London Electric Supply Co. Ltd which tended to dominate electricity supply in the eastern districts. Both were expanding and both were profitable: between 1919 and 1924 the number of the County of London's consumers doubled and company profits rose from £217,473 to £650,509.

During the twenties both electricity companies embarked on the construction of a new generation of colossal power stations. First was the County of London, whose massive Barking power station (fig. 141) was opened by King George V in 1925. In the words of the company chairman, Barking underlined that 'a great change has come over the industry. We have entered the era of big things.'[10] The London Power Company's equivalent was their scheme for a massive new power station at Battersea, to be linked to their existing station at Deptford, thus establishing economies of scale and more efficient central control of supply. Land was purchased at Battersea and in April 1927 the company applied to the Electricity Commissioners to build a 400MW station which when complete would provide more power than their existing nine power stations combined. Permission was granted in November, but the scheme had by this time become controversial, attracting the opposition of virtually everyone with London's public interests at heart: metropolitan boroughs, national newspapers, architects and even the Archbishop of Canterbury. The crux of the opposition was both ideological and environmental. This massive coal-burning station would discharge gritty soot and sulphurous fumes into the heart of London – a disastrously retrograde step for public health. Furthermore, in principle, this seemed to be a return to the bad old Victorian days, when unregulated private companies pursued their own commercial needs in flagrant disregard of the public good. Battersea Power Station became the Hungerford Bridge of the late twenties, a symbol of the ugliness brought by unregulated greed. The proposed station was a 'deplorable step backwards', a 'menace to London's buildings', a 'peril to public health'; it would endanger the art works at the Tate gallery, poison the population with sulphur and blacken London's buildings with soot. Critics conceded that new power stations were needed, but argued that they should be sited well beyond the centres of our great cities.

Despite the opposition, Battersea Power Station was built and began generating power in the early 1930s. Battersea is, arguably, the third of central London's great cathedrals of modernity that emerged from the debates of the twenties. Designed by Giles Gilbert Scott in 1929, the station was faced with brick rather than the white Portland stone which gave 55 Broadway and Broadcasting House their shimmering character. Battersea Power Station was a more earthbound affair. To the London Society, who were of course horrified at the prospect of this unplanned intrusion into the city centre, the building's industrial bluntness underlined that beauty and efficiency no longer went hand in hand. Battersea Power Station, to the Society, was the expression of soulless functionalism, a modern frame of mind which reinstated the old laws of utilitarian greed: 'the law of the machine age is inexorable and if we allow it to operate everywhere uncontrolled it will show us no pity . . . The law is that action taken for purely economic reasons no longer, as of old, creates new beauty, but destroys old beauty and substitutes modern ugliness.'[11]

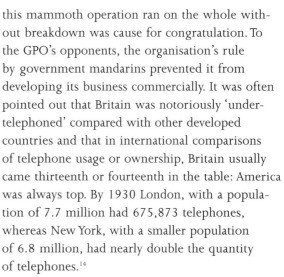

Communications

Machines that almost think!
The Illustrated London News, 1922[12]

By the twenties the General Post Office (GPO) was London's single biggest employer. In 1925 it employed 38,193 people in the London postal service and 9913 in the London telephone service.[13] The scale of its operation was massive. By the middle of the decade, the 1004 London post offices were handling thirteen million letters a month, fifty million parcels a year and £16 million worth of money and postal orders. London's telephone network comprised 4182 public call stations and 433,527 private phones (just under half Britain's total) from which around 900,000 outgoing and incoming calls were made yearly, all routed through the banks of operators in London's 102 manual telephone exchanges. With the exception of telegrams, which were losing ground to telephones, all the GPO's vital statistics were rising: more letters, more phone calls, more telephone exchanges needed, more staff required. To Post Office insiders, the fact that

this mammoth operation ran on the whole without breakdown was cause for congratulation. To the GPO's opponents, the organisation's rule by government mandarins prevented it from developing its business commercially. It was often pointed out that Britain was notoriously 'under-telephoned' compared with other developed countries and that in international comparisons of telephone usage or ownership, Britain usually came thirteenth or fourteenth in the table: America was always top. By 1930 London, with a population of 7.7 million had 675,873 telephones, whereas New York, with a smaller population of 6.8 million, had nearly double the quantity of telephones.[14]

Even the General Post Office's supporters in the twenties conceded that the organisation was a lumbering bureaucratic beast. Whereas Frank Pick at the Transport Combine set new standards for public relations, addressing the public through modern poster design and helpful signage, the GPO only addressed the public when imparting instructions in a ponderously superior tone of voice. 'How to pass and receive a telephone call,' instructed one broadsheet of 1923, telling subscribers that

144
Presentation casket, 1927
Glass and brass, 27 x 34 cm. Made by the Automatic Telephone Manufacturing Company to mark the opening of the London's first automated telephone exchange at Holborn in November 1927

145
Hand Combination Set, 1929
15 x 24 cm. Designed by an anonymous Siemens employee, it was Britain's first all-plastic phone, originally produced in coloured bakelite as well as black.

'on taking off the receiver, the called subscriber should not say "Hullo!" or "Who's there?" but should immediately announce his name.'[15] The broadsheet also ruled on the correct pronunciation to be used when speaking into the telephone 'if mistakes are to be avoided': 'five is pronounced as "FIFE", emphasising the consonants F.' But despite the old-fashioned paternalism, it was the General Post Office, more so than virtually any other twenties organisation, whose activities had the greatest long-term effect on the way Londoners ran their lives and used their city. It was GPO telephone engineers, as much as artists and writers, who really plugged London into the nerves of the world.

With such massive growth in their business, it is no surprise that automation was the issue of the day for both postal and telephone branches of the GPO, both of which reached significant automation milestones during the decade. In 1926 London's 'Mail Rail' opened, a driverless underground railway with automated machinery which took sacks of mail from Whitechapel to Paddington via the main sorting office at Mount Pleasant (fig. 142). In 1927 London's first automatic telephone exchange was opened at Holborn, enabling Londoners to dial numbers directly rather than asking the operator to connect them. Of the two advances the Mail Rail was the least impressive; indeed to some it was not impressive at all, demonstrating little more than the

GPO's bureaucratic inefficiency and technological backwardness. The criticisms stemmed from the long delay between 1913, when the system had been first authorised by the Treasury, and the Mail Rail's opening in 1926, by which time costs had escalated and the 1913 technology was virtually obsolete. 'Comment on this performance is surely needless,'[16] said Lord Wooton, a one-time Assistant Postmaster General whose unguarded aside in 1928 that the Post Office would, in his view, be more efficiently and economically managed under private enterprise caused a great commotion.

On the face of it the Post Office appeared also to have dragged its feet in modernising London's telephones. Britain's first automatic telephone exchange had been installed at Epsom in Surrey in 1912, yet it was not until 1927 that the first London exchange was converted from manual to automatic (fig. 144). The delay in this case was understandable: the magnitude and complexity of the London network made the conversion from manual to automatic with no interruptions of service a task of unique proportions, 'the telephoning of London . . . was the biggest single task which has ever faced the telephone industry in this country and the British Post Office. It meant a grave and irretrievable decision on policy, a carefully formulated and far-seeing plan, and years of work before that plan could be fulfilled.'[17]

The policy decision was also a technological one: which system would suit London's unique size and complexity? The small Epsom exchange of 1912 was a Strowger 'step-by-step' system. The only comparably complex network to London's was the New York telephone system which began to automate from 1919 using the 'panel' system developed by American manufacturers Western Electric. The panel system was an outstandingly ingenious piece of electrical equipment that could perform almost any telephonic task and was hailed as the nearest a machine had ever got to mimicking the human brain. The problem with the panel system was of course a political one: letting the London contract to a foreign firm would, in effect, render Britain's own telephone industry redundant. A politically and technologically satisfactory solution appeared when the Automatic Telephone Manufacturing Company, a British firm, proposed a hybrid system whereby the old step-by-step system was enhanced by a new device, the 'Director', which effectively produced the same miraculous effects as the panel system but without threatening existing manufacturing processes. In November 1922, the Post Office announced that the Director system was to be adopted for the automation of British exchanges, to the relief of Britain's telephone manufacturers: 'without the London contract, the industry in this country would have withered away.'[18]

From the public's point of view, the arrival of automated exchanges was indeed miraculous. Although some sentiment accompanied the departure of the telephone operators, the notion of dialling the number you wanted for yourself was universally welcomed, as was the Post Office's new design for the 'Hand Combination Set' introduced in 1929 (fig. 145). This classic design had been developed by the firm Siemens, whose engineer had reputedly

146
'K2' telephone kiosk, 1926
The standard 1926 kiosk designed by Giles Gilbert Scott (1880–1960)

been inspired by the sight of an Edwardian silver ink stand in a London shop window. Its novelty in 1929 was that it combined transmitter and receiver in one, as opposed to the old candlestick shaped apparatus (fig. 143) which continued to be offered to subscribers at a slightly cheaper rent. The new Hand Combination Set scored high on the fitness-for-purpose scale and it is no surprise to find its plain lines much admired by modernists.

The automation of Post Office operations in London also brought the need for new ways of mapping the city. London had been first divided into postal districts in 1857, but in 1917 a new system was introduced whereby each district was subdivided into smaller areas corresponding to delivery offices, each of which was assigned a number. The numbers were assigned alphabetically,

thus ensuring that the numbering made little sense in terms of London's real geography. The telephone map of London was almost as idiosyncratic. By 1920, there were around eighty manual exchanges in the Greater London area, but the prospect of automatic dialling meant that some names had to change to ensure that each exchange began with a unique three-letter sequence.[19] Thus HAMpstead and HAMmersmith could no longer co-exist; nor, thanks to the design of the dial which divided the alphabet into groups of three letters, could THAmes and VICtoria. Accordingly, new names began to appear on the telephone map. In 1924 Hammersmith became Riverside and part of Victoria became Franklin. More associations with famous men created Popesgrove (Twickenham) in 1926, Frobisher (Earl's Court) in 1927 and Flaxman (Chelsea) in 1929. The Docks transformed Plaistow into Albert and Wapping into Royal. North Ilford

became Valentine and Muswell Hill became Tudor. Later in the 1940s, Leytonstone chose the name Keystone, after the famous twenties silent film heroes, the Keystone Cops.

If the London Telephone Service altered the conceptual map of London, it also changed the capital's physical appearance through the arrival in 1926 of 'kiosk no. 2' (fig. 146), the red telephone box which was to assume iconic status as a symbol of London throughout the world.[20] The K2, designed by Giles Gilbert Scott, was initially unique to London in that it was an attempt to satisfy complaints from the metropolitan boroughs that the Post Office's standard 'kiosk no.1' was unattractive. The problem was taken on by the newly formed Royal Fine Art Commission who held a design competition and pronounced in February 1925 that they would be recommending to the Postmaster General the Gilbert Scott design as the most

147
The Bus Stop,
c.1924
William Roberts
(1895–1980),
watercolour, 26 x
75 cm. Probably
related to Roberts'
1924 commission
from Frank Pick to
create a large poster
for the British Empire
Exhibition on the
theme: The History
of the Omnibus

'suitable for erection in busy thoroughfares of large towns.' The K2 first appeared in 1926, and by 1929 around a thousand were installed on the capital's streets (a few were also installed in provincial cities but only on sites of suitable gravitas, such as next to town halls). Gilbert Scott's design was clearly classical in inspiration, yet also demonstrated a modern sense of simplicity and fitness for purpose. Although not as stripped back to basics as, say, Charles Holden might have produced, the K2 relies for its appeal as much on its geometry and the rhythms of its proportions as on its decorative detailing. The basic design adapted well to a more modernistic version, the K6, introduced in 1929 and given a more horizontal feel by realigning the glazing bars.

Interestingly, the red colour was not part of Gilbert Scott's original design. He initially conceived the kiosk as silver on the outside with a greenish blue inside. The General Post Office, however, insisted on Post Office red, which not only matched their post boxes but would give the new kiosks, they felt, a suitably authoritative appearance. The Royal Fine Art Commission approved and red was reinforced as London's official colour in October 1929 when the General Omnibus Company, part of the Combine, announced that after some unsuccessful trials with cream and yellow, all their London buses would in future be painted red. A correspondent to *The Times* tried to drum up support for dark green instead of 'hideous letterbox red', but to no avail.[21] By this time red buses had already become something of a London symbol (fig. 147): 'the typical London vehicle is undoubtedly the bus, a scarlet, thunderous monster, striking the eye at half a mile distant . . . It is part of the English passion for red, which foreigners find remarkable in so reticent a people.'[22]

Future

If the adult eyes of today could see [London] in the year 2000, they would doubtless find little to remind them of the London they knew; but for the people going about it, it will mean everything that our London means to us.

Thomas Burke, 1934[23]

In 1929 the film *High Treason*, directed by Maurice Elvey, opened as a British variation on the *Metropolis* vision of the future. Produced in a silent version as well as one of Britain's first talkies, *High Treason* was set in 1950 by which time the world was divided into two large superpowers: the Atlantic States, whose leaders tended to dress in white, and a Federated Europe, whose leaders dressed in black leather. The film's complicated plot revolves around the prevention of war following the assassination of the President of Europe and a subsequent air attack on New York. Footage of the real 1920s New York appears in the film but London, which figures heavily as the home of the World League of Peace and the frontier post created by the Channel Tunnel, is created through models (figs 149–50). The concerns of the twenties weave their way into the storyline, which features professional agitators, a League of Women and hedonistic dancing while the stormclouds gather. The sets include not only a bleak office in which rows of women sit at machines, but a glamorously High Society nightclub (fig. 148) whose automated jazz band consists of saxophones playing themselves without the need of musicians. In this vision of London's future, the Charing Cross bridge has at last been built, the Channel Tunnel is open – until it is blown up by agitators, the London skyline is crowded with skyscrapers, and there is universal gloom about international relations.

The gloomy prognosis offered by *High Treason* was not an unusual response to the events of 1929. In May the results of the 'mystery election', when the flapper vote was added into the democratic mix, produced Britain's second Labour administration – to the dismay of some. In July, to the dismay of others, the new Labour government refused asylum to Leon Trotsky, as a prelude to reopening diplomatic relations with the Soviet state. In October, the Wall Street crash sent shock waves through the world economy. By 1930 the mood had worsened. Aldous Huxley started work on his dystopian novel, *Brave New World*, in which the totalitarian World State subdues the individual with its inflexible belief in 'Community Identity Stability'. Lord Birkenhead's *The World in 2030AD* presented a less chilling but equally dramatic picture of the future. John Hargrave instructed the Kibbo Kift to put on their political green shirts. In October 1930, C.R.W. Nevinson exhibited 'Amongst the Nerves of the World' at London's Leicester Gallery (fig. 2).

With hindsight the unease that coloured the end of the twenties was more than justified by events to come: dark clouds were indeed ahead. However, despite the international situation, the fears that Huxley expressed for the extreme consequences of a social order that put the interests of the group above the interests of the individual were not to be realised, at least in Britain. And there were other reasons why optimism rather than pessimism about the future was an equally understandable response to the decade's end. London in 1929 was a cleaner, brighter and better managed city than it had ever been before. It was a more democratic city and had a remarkable transport system plus the foundations of a modern communications network. Although London remained in many respects as disorderly, diverse and illogical as it had ever been, the

148–50
High Treason, 1929
These stills show
the imagined world
of London in 1950:
the dance club with
its automated jazz
band behind the
floor-show, the
Channel Tunnel,
and theheadquarters
of the World League
of Peace at
Charing Cross.

potential for chaos had been to some extent stabilised by the underpinnings of a new cadre of public servants, armed with science and preaching the virtues of efficiency and self-discipline as a means towards humane ends.

London at the end of the decade remained the largest city in the western world, with only New York approaching London's population of 7.7 million. But the preceding ten years had also seen the capital come to a new understanding of Britain's place in the world. As we have seen, it was chiefly American influences that brought a looser, more outward-looking cultural character to London during the twenties. However, by the 1930s, the process of assimilating ideas from other countries, and indeed from levels other than the highbrow, had become part of London's natural order, or so it seemed to Thomas Burke in 1934:

> today we ride in taxis and buses through American streets and German streets and Scandinavian streets, and proudly show them to our visitors and say 'This is London'. For so strong is its power of absorbing alien importations into its essence and making them peculiar to itself, that today, when on all sides we see New York avenues and Stockholm buildings, we can still claim that their space and light are the expression of ourselves. London has woven them into its mighty fabric.[24]

What was true of the city's buildings and streets was also true of the ideas that had defined the energy and exuberance of twenties London. Democracy, Bolshevism, jazz, robots, skyscrapers, mass market, Empire Made and Home Rule: all passed into the thirties well woven into London's 'mighty fabric'. All were ready to spark off new explosions of energy in the decades to come.

151
**London's
Tramways
poster, 1927**
152 x 101 cm.
Designed by Leigh
Breton Studios for
the London County
Council

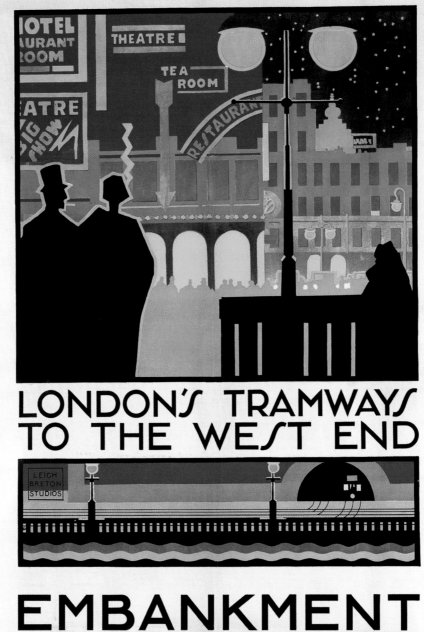

London's Jazz Age Buildings

This selection includes buildings mentioned in the book or which illustrate some of the points discussed. It does not include buildings which opened in the 1920s, but were designed in earlier decades, such as the County Hall.[1]

Britannic House, 1921–5
Finsbury Circus, EC2
Sir Edwin Lutyens (1869–1944)
The head office for the Anglo-Persian Oil Company. Britannic House looks like an Italian Renaissance palace on its top floors, but has a more modern feel in the plainer storeys beneath where the decoration is spread more sparsely. The outside appearance reflected the inside arrangement: the most important room, the boardroom, was placed on the top floor. The building was refurbished 1987–9 and is still the office of British Petroleum plc.

Midland Bank Head Office, 1924–37
Poultry, EC2
Sir Edwin Lutyens (1869–1944)
A massive steel-framed block given an Italian manner-ist exterior by its giant arches and heavy rusticated stone work. Inside, the central banking hall was designed as a palatial space lavishly finished with marble and African jadeite. The building is now the London head office for HSBC plc (the Hong Kong and Shanghai Banking Corporation).

Lloyds Bank Head Office, 1927–30
Cornhill, EC3
Sir John Burnet (1857–1938) and Campbell-Jones & Smithers
The building uses a conventional classical vocabulary with giant Corinthian columns set out in a grand manner. The site extends to Lombard Street but the façade here is plainer. As with all banking palaces of its day, the focus of the interior is a lavishly finished central banking hall with marble columns and mosaic floor designed to impress the public. The building is still Lloyds head office.

Bank of England, 1922–39
Threadneedle Street, EC2
Sir Herbert Baker (1862–1946)
Plans for extending the Bank had been first talked about in 1916, but it was not until the twenties that the rebuilding began. The structures inside the perimeter wall are Baker's, a piling-up of standard classical elements, all no doubt intended to convey gravitas and tradition. The exterior sculptures are by Sir Charles Wheeler (1892–1934).

Adelaide House, 1921–5
London Bridge Approach, EC3
Burnet & Tait
Built as offices and warehousing, this was London's highest commercial building (45 metres) when new, and visibly modern in style. Its steel-framed construction is reflected in its vertical lines and fashionable Egyptian detailing, both of which give it a 'Chicago' look. The building incorporated modern innovations such as a central ventilation system. The carved figure over the door is by Sir William Reid Dick (1878–1961). Adelaide House is now wholly offices.

Northcliffe House, 1925–7
Tudor Street, EC4
Ellis & Clarke
Built for Lord Rothermere's flagship newspaper, the *Daily Mail*, Northcliffe House had a conventional appearance, but its innovation lay on the inside. It was designed to house all the paper's departments under one roof, including the printing presses in the basement, the most automated in Britain at the time. The building has recently been refurbished as offices.

Daily Telegraph Building, 1928–31
Fleet St, EC4
Elcock & Sutcliffe with Thomas Tait (1882–1954)
The first of the American-style newspaper palaces in Fleet Street, built for new owners and incorporating a Director's penthouse suite on the upper floor. The fashionably loud design has been described as 'Neo-Graeco-Egyptian' and it was briefly the most prominent building in Fleet Street until it was upstaged by the black glass *Daily Express* building a few years later.

Summit House, 1925
Red Lion Square, WC1
Westwood & Emberton
Summit House served as a fireproof warehouse and offices for the clothing firm Austin Reed whose main retail showroom was a newly built traditional-looking block in Regent Street. Summit House looked efficiently modern with its glazed yellow tiles, geometric bulk and vertical lines emphasising the steel frame beneath. The building is now wholly offices and has recently been refurbished.

Grosvenor Housing Estate, 1928–30
Page Street and Vincent Street, SW1
Sir Edwin Lutyens (1869–1944)
A rehousing scheme for Westminster City Council on land donated by the Duke of Westminster. The estate blocks form Lutyens' least lavish and most modern building in that they are stripped back to geometric basics with no reference to older styles or architectural traditions, although the blocks are interspersed with small classical pavilions. The estate as a whole is still council-owned.

Crawford's Offices, 1930
233 High Holborn, WC1
Frederick Etchells (1887–1973) & Herbert A. Welch (1884–1953)
An extension for Crawford's Advertising Agency with a modernist feel created by the horizontal bands of windows interspersed with steel and concrete mullions. The black marble facings on the ground floor add a slight touch of luxury to what is otherwise an austere and functional building. The building remains in use as offices.

Bush House, 1922–5
Aldwych, WC2
Helmle & Corbett (other wings completed 1935)
A lavish and theatrical arrangement of classical elements fronting a large American office block. The sculpture group above the entrance is by Malvina Hoffman (1885–1966). In its early days Bush House housed many American firms and media organisations. Since 1940 Bush House has housed various branches of BBC radio, but the BBC plan to leave the building in 2003.

ICI House, 1928
Millbank, SW1
Sir Frank Baines (1877–1933)
A conventional head office block, with classical or Italianate details blown up to a large scale and spread over a steel-framed base. The block was the first element in a larger development and was joined in 1932 by Thames House, built alongside in the same overall style. By the 1930s Millbank was being seen as London's new office quarter thanks in part to the opening of Southwark Bridge.

Midland Bank, 1922
Piccadilly, SW1
Sir Edwin Lutyens (1869–1944)
An essay in 'Wrenaissance' architecture, faithfully
copying the style and spirit of Christopher Wren to
match his St James's Church next door. It was built for
the Midland Bank and remained in the hands of its
ssuccessor, HSBC plc, until last year. This was the first
of Lutyens' commissions from the Midland Bank and
it was carried out in co-operation with the firm of
Gotch and Saunders who specialised in bank interiors.

India House, 1928–30
Aldwych, WC2
Sir Herbert Baker (1862–1946)
A steel-framed, stone-faced building erected with
enormous speed and given an Indian flavour through
its decorative detailing. The building's appearance was
intended to underline that it had been commissioned
by the Indian government rather than the India Office
of the British government. Indian craftsmen carried
out some of the decorative work. India House is still
the home of the High Commission of India.

New Victoria Cinema, 1930
Vauxhall Bridge Road, SW1
W. E. Trent (1874–1948) & E. W. Lewis (1898–1977)
A building that looked to European rather than
American models in its horizontal emphasis spread
along the length of the building and chunky stylised
lettering: one of the building's architect's, E.W. Lewis,
had studied design in Germany. Inside, its lavish decoration was described at the time as resembling 'a fairy
palace under the sea'. The building is now the Apollo
Victoria theatre.

Grosvenor House, 1926–8
Park Lane, W1
Sir Edwin Lutyens (1869–1944) and L. Rome Guthrie
(1880–1958)
A development of luxury flats and a hotel for
property speculator A.O. Edwards on the site of the
old Grosvenor House. Both flats and hotel were
intended to cater for the American market, and the
building's appearance is American in spirit, although
the archi-tectural vocabulary is English neo-Georgian.
Gros-venor House is still a luxury hotel.

**London School of Hygiene and Tropical
Medicine, 1926–8**
Keppel Street, WC1
P. Morley Horder (fl. 1900–30) & Verner O. Rees
(1896–1966)
One of the first buildings in the new university
precinct in Bloomsbury. The building was intended
to house a new institute of public hygiene but has
since concentrated on tropical medicine. The slightly
austere 'stripped classical' building carries a rollcall of
famous British men of science around its top.

Devonshire House, 1924–6
Piccadilly, W1
Carrère & Hastings with Sir Charles Reilly
(1874–1948)
Designed by the American architects of the New York
Public Library, Devonshire House was a block of
luxury flats set above prestigious car showrooms and
built on the site of the demolished townhouse of the
Dukes of Devonshire. The block's overall bulk has an
American feel with the upper storeys set back from
the line of the street.

55 Broadway, 1927–9
Broadway, SW1
Charles Holden (1875–1960)

A massive American-scale cruciform block designed as headquarters for 'The Combine' which comprised London's General Omnibus and Underground Electric Railway companies. The building has minimal decoration save for some classical detailing and its famous sculptures by Eric Gill, Henry Moore and others set high above street level. Today it is the head office of Transport for London.

Liberty's Department Store, 1922–5
Regent Street, W1
E.T. and E.S. Hall

The frieze at the top of Liberty's East India House shows Britannia receiving the riches of the world. A more playful Eastern theme at street level has figures of the Buddha placed above the shop windows. The Buddha was a fashionable motif in the twenties and several featured in the rebuilt Regent Street. The building, which remains Liberty's flagship store, has recently been refurbished.

Liberty's Department Store, 1922–3
Great Marlborough Street, W1
E.T. and E.S. Hall

Tudor House is an ostentatiously English building, underlining Liberty's commitment to tradition and Arts and Crafts values. The wood used for the building was recycled from two eighteenth-century timber-framed ships: HMS Hindustan and HMS Impregnable. The interiors were modelled to resemble the courtyards of coaching inns. The exterior also included an elaborate Tudor-style clock.

Ideal House, 1927–9
Argyll Street, W1
S. Gordon Jeeves (1887–1964)

A showroom built for the American Radiator Company to match their New York headquarters, designed by Raymond Hood (1881–1934). An uncompromisingly modern building with polished black granite surfaces decorated with dramatic coloured enamels on metal fretwork plates. The original square building was extended in the 1930s and its overall impact has been slightly diluted by ground floor alterations.

Oxo Tower, 1928–30
Upper Ground, SE1
Albert W. Moore (1874–1965)

A concrete skyscraper which, at sixty-one metres, was briefly the tallest commercial building in London. It was also London's tallest advertisement in that the arrangement of the windows ingeniously promoted Oxo beef stock cubes, a product of the Leibig Meat Extract Co. which built Stamford Wharf on which the tower stands. Since 1996 the tower presides over set of restaurants, exhibition spaces and retail units.

Dickens & Jones Department Store, 1921
Regent Street, W1
Henry Tanner (1876–1947)

A standard steel-framed block, faced with stone but allowing for large plate glass windows at street level. The overall effect is similar to contemporary buildings nearby in Oxford Circus. The detailing is semi-Egyptian and semi-Roman. Dickens & Jones had been taken over by Harrod's in 1914. The building remains in use as a department store but its interiors have been altered over the years.

Ossulton Estate, 1927–31
Ossulton Street, NW1
London County Council Architects:
R. Minton Taylor & E.H. Parkes

Designed to set new standards for council housing, bridging the gap between functional tenement blocks and more well-appointed blocks of private luxury flats. The interiors aimed to set new standards of comfort. Externally, the 'white block' design reflected European models for workers' housing. The estate is still in council ownership and is currently being refurbished.

Arcadia Works, 1926–8
Hampstead Road, NW1
M.E. and O.H. Collins

Built as a state-of-the-art cigarette factory for the Carreras tobacco company. The building's façade was supposedly modelled on a temple to the Egyptian cat goddess Bubastis, a reference to the company's 'Black Cat' cigarettes. Inside it had an air-conditioning system and scientifically efficient production lines. Carreras moved out in 1959 and after a period as offices, the building was refurbished in 1999 for residential use.

Atkinson's, 1926
Old Bond Street, W1
E. Vincent Harris (1876–1971)

Designed as a shop for London's leading perfumery, this building is a mixture of medieval elements and fairy-tale fancy, including a tower with London's only carillon of bells. The interiors, which were intended to be seen from the street and 'form the window display', were designed by theatrical designer Norman Wilkinson and made use of cut glass, mirrors and fashionable 'feminine' colours of grey, pink and yellow.

Becontree Estate, 1919–37
Becontree Avenue, Romford
London County Council Architects
under R. Topham Forest

Showing one of the main roads in the estate's first section, begun in 1920 at the northwest corner of the site. By the end of the decade, 3700 houses had been erected in this section including some on land originally reserved for private development. The houses in this section were larger than those built later and were generally organised in blocks of four.

Bluebird Garage, 1924
King's Road, SW3
Robert Sharp (1884–1950)

Built for the Bluebird Motor Company and one of twenties London's largest garages, housing up to 300 cars along with workshops and waiting rooms. The steel-framed concrete building faced in white faience is typical of other large twenties garages, conveying functional efficiency together with fashionability. The Bluebird Garage was refurbished in the 1990s as a Conran restaurant.

Upper Feilde, 1922–4
Park Street and Upper Brook Street, W1
Wimperis, Simpson and Guthrie

A large block of mansion flats on the Grosvenor Estate in Mayfair. Its characteristic neo-Georgian design with red brick facing and stone classical details was intended to look elegant yet tastefully plain. Blocks of this type were typical of many of the flats built in Mayfair between the wars. They represent an attempt to develop the Georgian style of architecture for modern needs. Upper Feilde is still in residential use.

152
***Jazz Patterns*, 1927**
The cast of the play,
Jazz Patterns, at the
Everyman Theatre
in Hampstead:
Griselda Harvey,
Douglas Jefferies
and Mary Barton

Notes

Introduction

1 See, for example, Michael North, *Reading 1922: A Return to the Scene of the Modern* (New York & Oxford, 1999). As subsequent footnotes indicate, Michael North's ideas have been a strong influence on this account of the 1920s.

2 David Matless, 'Appropriate Geography: Patrick Abercrombie and the Energy of the World', *Journal of Design History* 6 (3), 1993, pp. 167–78

3 Lawrence Weaver, 'London's New Architecture' in St John Adcock, ed., *Wonderful London*, part 15 (London, 1926), p. 676

4 John Cournos, *Babel* (New York, 1922), pp. 124–5

Chapter 1

1 John Cournos, *Babel* (New York, 1922), pp. 88–9

2 Quoted in Robert Graves and Alan Hodge, *The Long Weekend* (London, 1940; repr. 1985), p. 172

3 Guglielmo Ferrero in *The Illustrated London News*, 27 March 1926

4 Thomas Burke, *London in My Time* (London, 1934), p. 132

5 H.G. Wells, *A Short History of the World* (London, 1922; repr. 1924), p. 257

6 *The Illustrated London News*, 12 January, 26 April, 3 May and 21 June 1926

7 Frank Rutter, *The British Empire Panels by Frank Brangwyn, R.A.* (Leigh on Sea, 1933; repr. 1937), p. 27

8 C.R.W. Nevinson, *Paint and Prejudice* (London, 1937), p. 205

9 *The Illustrated London News*, 6 May 1922

10 *The Illustrated London News*, 14 July 1923, referring to his speech made the previous year

11 *The Illustrated London News*, 30 June 1923

12 Clive Bell, *Since Cézanne* (London, 1922), pp. 203–4

13 Henry Woodd Nevinson, *Rough Islanders or the Natives of England* (London, 1930), p. 165

14 Wells, p. 260

15 *The Illustrated London News*, 19 January 1929

16 *The Illustrated London News*, 13 November 1926. See also *Punch*, 17 November 1926, p. 535 for a cartoon by L. Raven-Hill depicting two bookies deploring the totalisator because 'it destroys the yuman element', but welcoming the increase in betting that it will bring.

17 For accounts of Coué, see *The Illustrated London News*, 18 March, 8 and 15 April 1922.

18 For example, the writer Hamilton Fyfe, quoted in Michael North, *Reading 1922: A Return to the Scene of the Modern* (New York &
Oxford, 1999), p. 185 as part of a larger discussion about literary modernism, popular literature and the modern woman.

19 Earl of Birkenhead, *The World in 2030 AD* (London, 1930), p. 169

20 R.W.S. Mendl, *The Appeal of Jazz* (London, 1927), p. 186, quoted in E.D. Mackerness *A Social History of English Music* (London, 1966), p. 249

21 As quoted in Oleg Kerensky, *Anna Pavlova* (London, 1973), p. 104

22 Aldous Huxley, *Along the Road* (London, 1925), p. 251. See also 'Silence is Golden', an essay in *Do what you will* (London, 1929), pp. 52–61 for his account of seeing *The Jazz Singer* and being overcome with distaste.

23 Quoted in Martin Battersby, *The Decorative Twenties* (London, 1969), p. 146

24 Bell, p. 225. The chapter 'Plus de Jazz' is pp. 213–30.

25 Unidentified newspaper quoted in Norman MacDermott, *Everymania* (London, 1975), p. 79. See also fig. 152 here.

26 *The Musical Standard*, quoted in Mackerness, p. 250

27 Horace Wyndham, *Nights in London* (London, 1926), p. 63. The fifth chapter, 'Suburbia Unbends', has a good contemporary account of the Hammersmith Palais. For other details about London's clubs during the decade, see Victor MacClure, *How to be Happy in London* (London, 1926) and G.H. Fosdyke Nichols, 'A Round of the Night Clubs' in St John Adcock, ed., *Wonderful London*, part 3 (London, 1926), pp. 940–52.

28 *The Times*, 9 September 1923, p. 17

29 For other accounts of the arrival of jazz in Britain, see Ross McKibbin, *Classes and Cultures: England 1918–51* (Oxford, 1998), Jim Godbolt, *A History of Jazz in Britain, 1919–50* (London, 1986) and Howard Rye, 'Fearsome Means of Discord: Early Encounters with Black Jazz' in Paul Oliver, ed., *Black Music in Britain* (Buckingham, 1990), pp. 45–57.

30 The painting is reproduced in the *Royal Academy Illustrated*, 1926. Disappointed at the painting's removal, Souter destroyed the original but later in his life painted a smaller version, which is reproduced in Joan M. Matthew, *J.B. Souter, 1890–1971* (Perth, 1990). Matthew's book also includes a fuller account of the incident at the Royal Academy.

31 *Revue Romande*, 19 October 1919, quoted in John Chiltern, *Sidney Bechet: The Wizard of Jazz* (New York, 1966), p. 40

32 Cournos, p. 243: 'You struck a ball out of America and it shot in a straight line to
France, went off at an angle to England, and back to America. Europe was Europeanising America, America was Americanising Europe.'

Chapter 2

1 Glyn Roberts, *I Take this City* (London, 1933), p. 61

2 *The Illustrated London News*, 4 September 1926

3 Thomas Burke, *London in My Time* (London, 1934), p. 35

4 Charles Higham, *Advertising: Its Use and Abuse* (London, 1925), p. 7

5 Lawrence Weaver, 'The Modern Architecture of London', in St John Adcock, ed., *Wonderful London*, part 15 (London, 1926), p. 677

6 John Skeaping, *Drawn from Life: An Autobiography* (London, 1977), p. 88

7 Ross McKibbin, *Classes and Cultures: England 1918–51* (Oxford, 1998), p. 31

8 Nancy Cunard, *Negro* (London, 1934), p. 75

9 Nina Hamnett, *Is She a Lady? A problem in autobiography* (London, 1955), p. 59

10 H.M.E. Clamp, *The Great God Jazz* (London, n.d. but c.1924), p. 68. Clamp's novel goes to some length to disguise thinly its source material: the Society protagonists live in Mayfair's 'Bulkley Square' and laugh at modern art by 'Latisse', 'Sakst' and 'Eckstein'.

11 *The Times*, 1 March 1928. The Hartnell wedding dress was also illustrated in *The Graphic*, 26 May 1928.

12 Paul Cohen-Portheim, *England the Unknown Isle* (London, 1930), quoted in McKibbin, p. 34

13 'Yorick' [Sheridan Bickers], 'To our readers', *The Theatre World* 1 (1925), p. 2

14 *The Illustrated London News*, 27 March 1926

15 Burke, p. 42

16 H.V. Morton, *The Spell of London* (London, 1926), p. 61

17 Constance Harris, *The Use of Leisure in Bethnal Green: A Survey of Social Conditions in the Borough, 1925–6* (London, 1927), pp. 50–51

18 G.K. Chesterton, 'The New Journalism', *The Illustrated London News*, 7 February 1925

19 Quoted in Goronwy Rees, *St Michael: A History of Marks & Spencer* (London, 1960; repr. 1973), pp. 73–4

20 Burke, p. 73

21 Quoted in Rees, p. 74. The details in the two following paragraphs are all taken from this source: pp. 67–84.

22 Florence A. Kirkpatrick, 'Shopping East and West', in St John Adcock, ed., *Wonderful London*, part 5 (London, 1926), p. 243

23 The details in this and the following paragraph are taken from Peter Bird, *The First Food*

Empire: A History of J. Lyons & Co. (Chichester, 2000), pp. 98–107, 142–7

24 Ronald Bousquet Browne, 'T.B. Browne Ltd. The first 100 Years', undated typescript (c.1975) in the History of Advertising Trust Archive: 'Advertising Agencies: B'

25 *The Illustrated London News*, 12 July 1924

26 Information about Benson's comes from Brian Sibley, *The Book of Guinness Advertising* (London, 1985), pp. 38–40 and printed ephemera in the History of Advertising Trust Archive. The firm's extensive archive of posters survives in the collections of the Museum of London and the Victoria & Albert Museum.

27 *The Illustrated London News*, 29 April 1922

28 *The Illustrated London News*, 5 December 1925

29 John Trench, writing in the programme for Bensons Centenary Lunch 1993, in the History of Advertising Trust Archive: 'Advertising agencies: B'.

Chapter 3

1 J.M. Keynes, *A Short View of Russia* (London, 1925), p. 28

2 Clive Bell, *Since Cézanne* (London, 1922), p. 145

3 The phrase is from the painter Jacques Emile Blanche, quoted in David Chadd and John Gage, *The Diaghilev Ballet in England* (Norwich, 1979), which provides a detailed account of the company's activities in England and is the basis for the summary provided here. See also Cyril W. Beaumont, *The Diaghilev Ballet in London: A Personal Record* (London, 1940).

4 See *Punch*, 23 June 1926, p. 663. A cartoon by Bernard Partridge shows Mme Bolshova showering coins into the sack of A.J. Cook, the miners' leader.

5 *Evening Standard*, 26 November 1923, names Battersea as one of the capital's 'four red boroughs' without identifying the other three. They were almost certainly Bethnal Green, Poplar and probably Stepney.

6 From a review by W.T. Turner in *The Illustrated London News*, 23 July 1927

7 'Politics' in Max Beerbohm, *A Survey* (London, 1921), plate 27. According to Rupert Hart-Davis, *A Catalogue of the Caricatures of Max Beerbohm* (London, 1972), the original drawing was exhibited at the Leicester Gallery in May 1921.

8 Clive Bell, *Old Friends* (London, 1956), quoted in Chadd and Gage, p. 23

9 Harold Acton, *Memoirs of an Aesthete* (London, 1948), quoted in Chadd and Gage, p. 29

10 Quotations in this paragraph and the next are taken from Chadd and Gage, pp. 40–43

11 *The Illustrated London News*, 13 December 1924

12 *Punch*, 28 April 1920, p. 327. The cartoon is by J.H. Dowd.

13 Bell, *Since Cézanne*, pp. 128–9

14 See Brandon Taylor, *Art for the Nation* (Manchester, 1999), pp. 132–66, for a full discussion of this point.

15 *The Graphic*, 28 July 1928: 'Miss Edith Sitwell presents a genius?'

16 *Daily Telegraph*, 15 June 1925, referring to Shapurji Saklatvala, quoted in Mike Squires, *Saklatvala: A Political Biography* (London, 1990), p. 124

17 *Punch*, 13 January 1926, p. 41. The cartoon is by J.H. Thorpe.

18 *The Times*, 2 December 1929. According to the Communist Party's own records, membership reached 10,000 in 1926, but fell to 3000 in 1929.

19 *The Illustrated London News*, 28 May 1921

20 Keynes, p. 25

21 For further information on Saklatvala, see Squires (above), Marc Wadsworth, *Comrade Sak: A Political Biography* (London, 1998) and Sehri Saklatvala, *The Fifth Commandment* (London, 1991), which is also available at www.maze-in.com/saklatvala.

22 Glyn Roberts, *I Take This City* (London, 1933), pp. 15–16

23 Public Record Office: MEPO 3/296 has the police report of the incident.

24 Keynes, p. 11

25 See, for example, *The Illustrated London News*, 12 April 1919, 16 October 1920, 14 November 1925 and 25 June 1927.

26 Quoted in Richard Bennett, *A Picture of the Twenties* (London, 1961), p. 168

27 A speech at the Queen's Hall, reported in *The Illustrated London News*, 11 October 1924

28 Mary Agnes Hamilton, *J. Ramsay MacDonald* (London, 1929), p. 245

29 *The Illustrated London News*, 26 January 1924

Chapter 4

1 C.G. Lawrence, ed., *Official Guide: The British Empire Exhibition* (London, 1924), p. 103

2 Advertisement in *The Times*, 9 November 1923, for Lines Bros, toy manufacturers

3 Lawrence, p. 13

4 Quoted in Stephen Constantine, *Buy & Build: The Advertising Posters of the Empire Marketing Board* (London, 1986), p. 17.

5 *The Illustrated London News*, 3 October 1925

6 *The Illustrated London News*, 25 July 1925

7 The information about these societies is taken from Peter Fryer, *Staying Power: The History of Black People in Britain* (London, 1984), chapters 9–10, and Rozina Visram, *Asians in Britain: 400 Years of History* (London, 2002), chapters 7–10, both of which provide a detailed discussion of the groups involved.

8 *The Illustrated London News*, 24 October 1925, printed a small photograph of the Prince dressed 'as a young woman' in order to take part in a farce performed aboard ship.

9 See Michael North, *Reading 1922: A Return to the Scene of the Modern* (New York and Oxford, 1999), pp. 110–19 for an interesting discussion of the Prince and his dress on his world tours.

10 The original photograph of the Prince on holiday at Biarritz was printed in *The Illustrated London News*, 12 April 1924. The oil painting was copied directly from the photograph and a colour reproduction of the painting was given away free with *The Illustrated London News* Christmas issue, 12 December 1925.

11 The polo portrait was presented to Manchester City Art Gallery. *Royal Friends* was presented to Leeds City Art Gallery in 1926.

12 Quoted in *The Illustrated London News*, 31 May 1924

13 Report on His Majesty's Government Participation in the British Empire Exhibition, 1924/5. Public Record Office: BT 60/14/2

14 The account of the construction of Wembley is largely taken from *British Empire Exhibition 1924* (Wembley History Society Journal, 1974), a special edition compiled from several articles previously published in the W.H.S. Journal. For details about the individual exhibits at Wembley, see D.R. Knight and A.D. Sabey, *The Lion Roars at Wembley* (London, 1984).

15 *The Times*, 21 April 1924

16 From an advertisement for the Concrete Utilities Bureau on the back cover of London County Council, *Housing: Being one of a series of popular handbooks on the London County Council and what it does for London* (London, 1924)

17 This account is taken from Andy Pendlebury and Giles Allen in *Stamp History 1* (1996), an information sheet distributed by Consignia Heritage Services.

18 Details about the government pavilion, stadium and pageant are taken from Public Record Office: BT 60/14/2

19 Charles Higham, *Advertising: Its Use and Abuse* (London, 1925), pp. 220–21

20 Higham, p. 216. See also chapter 11, 'The Advertising of Ideas'.

21 For the arguments behind the foundation of the British Institute of Industrial Arts, see the Public Record Office: ED24/601 which includes the original 'vision' outlined in 1914 by Hubert Llewellyn Smith. It also contains the responses, including the view of Sir C.H. Read of the British Museum that

the scheme 'is more likely to succeed without state control. People can no more be made artistic than they can be made sober by Act of Parliament.'

22 *The Illustrated London News*, 2 October 1920. See also 20 May 1922 for a eulogistic account of the Chelsea potteries of Charles Vyse and Gwendolen Parnell.

23 The best account of the Empire Marketing Board's promotional activities is Stephen Constantine, *Buy & Build: The Advertising Posters of the Empire Marketing Board* (London, 1986). The account here is based on this and files in the Public Record Office, particularly CO 760/26.

24 First Report of the Empire Marketing Board, July 1926, p. 2. Public Record Office: CO 323/962/7

25 The quotation at the end of the paragraph is from *The Illustrated London News*, 14 July 1923, which illustrates the first batch of his posters. See also the issues of 21 July 1923 and 10 May 1924 for further images.

26 Public Record Office: Empire CO 760/26

27 *Advertising Display*, a supplement to *The Advertisers Weekly*, 26 December 1926. A copy is in CO 758/104/1.

28 Public Record Office: CO 760/26, 'Inspectors' report on retail display materials', 8 November 1928

Chapter 5

1 Stanley Baldwin, Speech given at the Annual Dinner of the Royal Society of St George at the Hotel Cecil, 6 May 1924, reproduced in *On England* (London, 1933), pp. 5–6

2 John Hargrave, *The Confession of the Kibbo Kift* (London, 1927), p. 250

3 *The Times*, 1 March 1928. See also *The Illustrated London News*, 10 March 1928, which illustrates Gill's sculptures and praises his 'distinctly English character'.

4 Professor L.P. Elwell-Smith, Introduction to John Hargrave, *The Confession of the Kibbo Kift* (London, 1927; facsimile 1979), p. 1

5 Hargrave, p. 250. The account of the Kibbo Kift here is largely based on material deposited in the Museum of London. The other sources of information about the Kibbo Kift are the Kindred's own website, www.enduser.co.uk/kibbokift, and Mark Drakeford, *Social Movements and their Supporters: The Green Shirts in England* (London, 1997). The movement's archive is deposited at the London School of Economics and the Museum of London, the former holding the main paper archive, the latter holding photographs, artwork, costumes, printed material and the Kinlog, the movement's official chronicle.

6 Hargrave, p. 11

7 Hargrave, p. 57

8 Hargrave, p. 74

9 Quoted in Drakeford, p. 57. The speaker was Vera Chapman, 'Lavengri'.

10 Quoted in Drakeford, p. 34. The quote is from August 1923.

11 Quoted in Drakeford, p. 75

12 The Kindred's links to experimental education of the time were reflected in the presence on its Advisory Council of John Howard Whitehouse, founder of Bembridge School on the Isle of Wight. Several members were connected with other progressive schools, notably the Modern School at Matlock. In April 1929 the Kibbo Kift presented an exhibition of their educational work at the Whitechapel Art Gallery.

13 Hargrave, pp. 99–100 for all the quotes in this paragraph

14 Hargrave, p. 315

15 Hargrave, p. 216

16 Hargrave, p. 120

17 Hargrave, p. 222

18 Hargrave, pp. 72–3

19 The British Monomark was established in 1925 by arrangement with the General Post Office to realise an idea supposedly invented by William Morris. It provided a kind of poste restante service based on, according to its advertisements, 'a science of identity'. Registered firms were given a cryptic postal address (the Kibbo Kift's address was 'BM/Kift London WC1') and the system was promoted as a modern marketing tool: a Monomark advertisement in *The Illustrated London News*, 1 May 1926, promised that 'From Sydney to the Argentine, from China to Peru. There's a marketplace for British goods and a monomark for you.'

20 Hargrave, p. 309

21 Hargrave, p. 222

22 Quoted in Drakeford, p. 56

23 Hargrave, p. 87

24 Hargrave, p. 311

25 Quotations in this paragraph are taken from Chris Judge Smith, 'White Fox: a biographical note' (1995), reproduced on the Kibbo Kift website and from Drakeford, pp. 87–8.

26 Hargrave, p. 269

27 Quoted by Smith on the Kibbo Kift website

28 Frank Pick, 'The Art of the Street', *The Journal of the London Society* 64, 1923, p. 10

29 Kibbo Kift cartoon: no. 60, 9 March 1928. Entitled 'A choice of Gods', the cartoon contrasted 'Life/ Play/Time' with 'Machine/Thump/Robot/R.S.S.R' and proclaimed 'Machine shall be the slave of man but we will not slave for machine.'

30 Hargrave, pp. 179–80

31 Hargrave, p. 177

32 Hargrave, p. 38

33 Hargrave, p. 44

34 John Hargrave, *Social Credit Clearly Explained* (London, 1945), p. 60

35 Hargrave, p. 250

36 Hargrave, p. 167

37 See David Matless, 'Appropriate Geography: Patrick Abercrombie and the Energy of the World', *Journal of Design History* 6 (3), 1993, pp. 167–78

Chapter 6

1 Alfred Noyes, 'The Magic of London' in St John Adcock, ed., *Wonderful London*, part 1 (London, 1926), p. 4

2 Sir Lawrence Weaver, 'London's New Architecture', in Adcock, part 15, p. 676

3 Thomas Burke, *London in My Time* (London, 1934), p. 20

4 Weaver, p. 676

5 Burke, pp.16–17

6 Professor Adshead, 'Central London' in Sir Aston Webb, ed., *London of the Future* (London, 1921), p. 151

7 Burke, p. 118

8 Burke, p. 127

9 H.J. Leaning in *The Journal of the London Society* 28, 1928, p. 1

10 See *London of the Future* (above) which contains several diatribes against the railways. See also H.J. Leaning, 'London Railway reconstruction' (pp. 69–92) for various 'rationalisation' schemes.

11 Arthur Keen, *Charing Cross Bridge* (London, 1930), p. v. This book provides a good summary of the debates surrounding London's inner city bridges. See also a famous *Punch* cartoon by Frank Reynolds, 3 January 1923, in which the Spirit of Ugliness proudly contemplates Hungerford Bridge as 'my masterpiece'.

12 Glyn Roberts, *I Take This City* (London, 1933), p. 272

13 Burke, p. 55

14 These statistics are all taken from London County Council, *London Statistics*, vol. 30, 1924–5 (London, 1926).

15 Barry Pain, 'London Types' in Adcock, part 2, p. 51

16 *Broken Blossoms or the Yellow Man and the Girl*, directed by D.W. Griffith, was released in 1919.

17 C.P. Hawkes, *The London Comedy* (London and Boston, 1925), p. 99

18 This information is taken from John Chiltern, *Sidney Bechet: The Wizard of Jazz* (London, 1987; repr. New York, 1996), pp. 46–54. See also Howard Rye, 'Fearsome Means of Discord:

Early Encounters with Black Jazz' in Paul Oliver, ed., *Black Music in Britain* (Buckingham, 1990), pp. 45–57 for further details of black musicians in London.

19 Roberts, p. 275

20 Hawkes, p. 98

21 For details of black and Asian individuals and societies in London, see Peter Fryer, *Staying Power: The History of Black People in Britain* (London, 1984), chapter 10; Rozina Visram, *Asians in Britain: 400 Years of History* (London, 2002), chapters 7–10; and Susan Okokon, *Black Londoners 1880–90* (Stroud, 1998)

22 Chiltern, p. 47

23 The 1919 race riots are covered more fully in Fryer, pp. 298–316 and Visram, pp. 198–201.

24 Burke, p. 56

25 Public Record Office: HO 45/24748

26 A. Emil Davies, *The Story of the London County Council* (London, 1925), p. 12

27 Raymond Unwin, 'Some thoughts on the development of London' in Webb, p. 187.

28 Quoted in James Gillespie, 'Municipalism, Monopoly and Management: The Demise of Socialism in One Country, 1918–1933' in Andrew Saint, ed., *Politics and the People of London: The London County Council, 1889–1965* (London, 1989), pp. 103–25

29 Davies, p. 14

30 Davies, p. 51

31 L. Haden Guest, ed., *The New Education* (London, 1920), p. 4. The book is a discussion of the new provisions for London's education enabled by the 1918 Education Act.

32 The London County Council minutes of 7 February 1922 recorded that students at the Central School should be asked to supply 'pictorial posters' for use inside tramcars, alongside 'propaganda posters' to advertise the service. The nature of the pictorial posters remains unclear except that they were to be 'designed so as to be suitable for varying times of year'. Many of the 'propaganda posters' have survived in various public collections including the Museum of London's. The artwork for all the tramway posters 1922–33 survives at London Metropolitan Archives: LCC/ TWYS /01.

33 Sir Henry Haward, *The London County Council from Within* (London, 1932), p. 142. All the following references to housing bonds are also from this source.

34 The details of Becontree here are taken from the London County Council, *Housing, with Particular Reference to Post-war Housing Schemes* (London, 1928), pp. 67–77.

35 Quoted in Antonia Rubinstein, ed., *Just Like the Country: Memories of London Families who Settled the New Cottage Estates, 1919–39* (London, 1991), p. 60

36 Rubinstein, pp. 7 and 94

Chapter 7

1 Stephen Leacock, *Journal of the London Society* 83, 1922, p. 5

2 London Society, 'Exhibit of Maps shewing the occupation of the various boroughs of London', pamphlet [London, 1923], p. 3

3 Raymond Unwin, 'Some thoughts on the development of London' in Sir Aston Webb, ed., *London of the Future* (London, 1921), p. 177

4 Clough Williams-Ellis, *England and the Octopus* (London, 1928)

5 W.E. Vernon Crompton, 'The Ideal Street', *Journal of the London Society* 21, 1919, p. 10

6 Harold S. Clunn, *The Face of London* (Third edn, London, 1932), p. 13

7 C.P. Hawkes, *The London Comedy* (London and Boston, 1925), p. 21

8 London Society, 'Exhibit of Maps . . .', p. 3

9 London Society, *Development Plan of Greater London prepared during the Great War, 1914–18* (London, 1918)

10 London Society, 'Exhibit of Maps . . .', p. 3

11 *Journal of the London Society* 47, 1922, p. 6.

12 Hawkes, p. 25

13 Dean Inge, *Journal of the London Society* 39, 1921, p. 4. The remark was made as part of a discussion on what London would be like in 1971. Inge, a traditionalist whose ideal city was Auckland in New Zealand, thought London would be spiritually better off if the city was smaller and poorer in fifty years time.

14 Arthur J. Penty, 'Where Architecture is Alive, III', *Architect: The Journal of the Society of Architects* 3 (18), 1924–5, p. 120

15 The Ian Strang drawing was reproduced as plate 42 of John Drinkwater, ed., *The Artist's London as seen in Eighty Contemporary Pictures* (London, 1924) to illustrate 'the lively interest of contemporary artists' in demolition, steel girders and Scotch cranes. Strang's etching of the same subject appeared in E. Beresford Chancellor, *Disappearing London* (London, 1927).

16 See, for example, *The Illustrated London News*: 'Colossal Architecture: Remarkable Buildings of Modern America' (9 April 1927); 'A Fairy Tale City of Titan Towers' (2 January 1926); 'The World's Largest Skyscraper: Rome to Outsoar New York' (24 January 1925) reporting Mussolini's plans for a 1110-foot-high (336m) building.

17 Harvey Corbett, quoted in *Journal of the London Society* 50, 1922, p. 3, reporting an interview published in *American Architect*, 18 January 1922.

18 The souvenir brochure commemorating the opening by King George V, 8 July 1930, p. 3.

19 *Journal of the London Society* 154, 1930, pp. 185–6

20 Hawkes, pp. 25–6

21 James Laver, 'Last Week in Babylon' in John Drinkwater, ed., *The Artist's London as seen in Eighty Contemporary Pictures* (London, 1924), p. xxvi

22 The scheme is illustrated in an unsourced cutting, possibly a fundraising leaflet, dated July 1916 in the Power Collection, Museum of London, Box reference: Strand I/ Aldwych

23 See Christopher Simon Sykes, *Private Palaces: Life in the Great London Houses* (London, 1985), pp. 321–40 for more details about the loss of the great Mayfair houses between the wars.

24 The RIBA drawings collection contains four small sketches for this scheme. Besides the perspective shown, there are plans of the blocks, one of which is reproduced in Duncan Simpson, *C.F.A.Voysey: An Architect of Individuality* (London, 1979) which also discusses the tower blocks in more detail, pp. 134–7.

25 Sir Martin Conway, 'London as I should like to see it', *Journal of the London Society* 25, 1920, p. 6

26 *The Illustrated London News*, 26 August 1922

27 See Trystan Edwards, 'The Clash of Colour or the Moor of Argyll Street', *Architectural Review* 65, 1929, pp. 289–95 for an amusing discussion of the two buildings.

28 Much of the information here is taken from F.H.W. Sheppard, *Survey of London: The Grosvenor Estates in Mayfair*, part 1, vol. 39 (London, 1977), pp. 161–70

29 The hotel opened in May 1929 and was heavily advertised. See, for example, *The Illustrated London News*, 18 May and 12 October 1929.

30 Quoted in Sheppard, p. 165

31 Iain S. Black, 'Rebuilding the Heart of Empire: Bank Headquarters in the City of London, 1919–39' in Dana Arnold, ed., *The Metropolis and Its Image: Constructing Identities for London* (Oxford, 1999), pp. 127–52

32 Sir Lawrence Weaver, 'London's New Architecture' in St John Adcock, ed., *Wonderful London*, part 15 (London, 1926), p. 684

33 Frank Pick, 'The Art of the Street as Illustrated in London', *Journal of the London Society* 64, 1923, p. 10

34 Professor Adshead, 'Central London' in Webb, p. 150

35 *The Illustrated London News*, 1 March 1924 illustrates the bridge proposed for Oxford Circus. Yarrow had offered to bear all the costs for erecting the flyover if the idea was subsequently adopted. He also proposed a bridge for the junction between Holborn and Kingsway.

36 Traffic statistics are taken from London County Council, *London Statistics*, vol. 30, 1924–5 (London, 1926)

37 For accounts of the Regent Street rebuilding, see Hermione Hobhouse, *A History of Regent Street* (London, 1975); F.H.W. Sheppard, ed., *Survey of London: Parish of St James Westminster, part two: north of Piccadilly*, vol. 31 (London, 1963), pp. 85–100; Erika Rappaport, 'Art, commerce or Empire: The rebuilding of Regent Street', *History Workshop Journal*, Spring 2002, pp. 95–157

38 Thomas Burke, *London in My Time* (London, 1934), p. 25. See also Sheppard's *Survey of London* (above) on 'Illuminated Advertising in Piccadilly Circus', pp. 97–100 for an account of the debate.

39 For pictures of the Piccadilly Circus tube station, see *The Illustrated London News*, 15 December 1928.

Chapter 8

1 J.C.W. Reith, *Broadcast over Britain* (London, 1924), p. 220. The chimes of Big Ben were first broadcast in 1923 and the Greenwich Mean Time pips in 1924.

2 Reith, p. 217

3 R.H. Tawney, *The Acquisitive Society* (London, 1921; repr. 1943), pp. 150–51

4 Quoted in Brian Hanson, 'Singing the Body Electric with Charles Holden', *Architectural Review*, December 1975, p. 351

5 The best account of 55 Broadway and its public sculptures is Richard Cork, *Art Beyond the Gallery in Early Twentieth-Century England* (New Haven and London, 1985), pp. 248–96

6 All quotations from Cork, pp. 290–91

7 The design for the BBC's new headquarters was unveiled in November 1928 and widely reported: see, for example, *The Illustrated London News*, 1 December 1928

8 Sir Evelyn Murray, *The Post Office* (London, 1927), p. 117. For an account of the early yeras of the BBC, see Asa Briggs, *The Birth of Broadcasting* (London, 1961).

9 For an account of electricity provision in twenties London, see James Gillespie, 'Municipalism, Monopoly and Management: The Demise of Socialism in One Country, 1918–1933' in Andrew Saint, ed., *Politics and the People of London: The London County Council, 1889–1965* (London,. 1989), pp. 112–16. The London County Council's *London Statistics* annuals list the many authorised distributors of electricity and their areas of supply.

10 County of London Electricity Company, *Opening of the Company's New Power House at Creekmouth, Barking, by His Majesty King George V on 19 May 1925* (London, 1925), p. 16.

11 George Trevelyan, quoted in *Journal of the London Society* 139, 1929, p. 6. See also other editions of the journal and the national press over the summer of 1929 when the campaign against the power station was at its height.

12 *The Illustrated London News*, 25 November 1922. Headline above a feature on automatic telephone exchanges

13 GPO statistics taken from London County Council, *London Statistics*, vol. 30, 1924–5 (London, 1926).

14 Lord Wooton, *Post Office Reform* (London, 1932), p. 121, diagram II

15 'How to Pay and receive a telephone call', broadsheet, October 1923

16 Wooton, p. 89. See also the whole of chapter 3, 'The Mails'.

17 J.H. Robertson, *The Story of the Telephone* (London, 1947), p. 148

18 Robertson, p. 176

19 Information about telephone exchange names is taken from an unpublished text by Neil Johannessen of British Telecom.

20 For good accounts of the red phonebox, see British Telecom Education Service (Neil Johannessen), *Britain's Public Payphones: A Social History* (London, 1984) and Gavin Stamp, *Telephone Boxes* (London, 1989).

21 *The Times*, 10 December 1929. On the other hand, a letter printed in *The Times* on 21 October 1929 had complained about the 'sickly yellow' used in the trials and called for the 'brilliant scarlet' to be reinstated.

22 James Laver, 'Last Week in Babylon' in John Drinkwater, ed., *The Artist's London as seen in Eighty Contemporary Pictures* (London, 1924), p. xxvi

23 Thomas Burke, *London in My Time* (London, 1934), p. 251

24 Burke, pp. 38–9

Appendix

1 Dates given are for individual architects, not for partnerships or firms. Further details about most of the buildings listed here can be found in the various editions of Nikolaus Pevsner's *The Buildings of England* series.

Twenties London: A Chronology

1918

February: The Representation of the People Act triples the size of the British electorate by giving the vote to all men over the age of twenty-one and all women over the age of thirty. Nearly two million Londoners are now eligible to vote.

November: The First World War effectively ends with the Armistice.

1919

July: Following the signing of the Versailles Peace Treaty, London sees the official Victory March and many local peace celebrations.

December: Nancy, Lady Astor becomes the first woman to take a seat in the British parliament. The Irish Republican Army is founded to fight for Home Rule for Ireland. The London Labour Party manifesto calls for Home Rule for London.

1920

July: The Communist Party of Great Britain is founded in London. The London County Council bans 'aliens' from most council jobs.

November: The cenotaph is unveiled in Whitehall as the nation's memorial to its war dead.

December: The Irish Partition Bill proposes a solution to the increasingly violent Irish situation by dividing the country into two separate states.

1921

January–June: Unemployment in Britain soars from just under one million to over two million.

March: The coal strike threatens to turn into a general strike and the government declares a state of emergency. Britain's first birth control clinic, the idea of Dr Marie Stopes, opens in the Holloway Road, London.

June: The new Southwark Bridge is opened by King George V.

September: Charlie Chaplin, the London-born film star now based in Hollywood, visits his home city and is mobbed by adoring crowds.

1922

November: The British Broadcasting Company begins regular radio broadcasts from its London station '2LO' transmitting from the top of Marconi House in the Strand. The opening of Tutankhamen's tomb in Egypt creates a media frenzy.

December: Ireland is officially divided into two separately governed states: the Irish Free State in the south and the Northern province of Ulster which remains under British rule.

1923

April: 300,000 football fans pack the new Wembley Stadium to see the first Wembley Cup final: Bolton Wanderers beat West Ham United, 2–0.

July: The Matrimonial Causes Act allows a wife to petition for divorce on the grounds of adultery: previously only the husband could cite adultery as a reason.

November: The first transatlantic radio broadcast between London and New York.

1924

January: Britain's first Labour government is formed by Ramsay MacDonald. In the election the preceding December, the turnout in London was 60%.

April: The British Empire Exhibition is opened at Wembley by King George V. Over ten million visitors see the event before it closes in September.

June: The London Road Traffic Act brings some much needed regulation to the unco-ordinated competition of private bus and tram operators in central London.

October: The Labour government is brought down by the Zinoviev letter scandal. In the subsequent election, the Conservatives win a massive victory: turnout in London is 71%.

1925

January: The statue of Eros is removed from Piccadilly Circus in preparation for the construction of an enormous new tube station: Eros will be absent for six years.

April: The Chancellor of the Exchequer, Winston Churchill, returns Britain to the Gold Standard, a major change of direction for Britain's economy.

May: A large section of the Great West Road in west London is opened by King George V.

November: Twelve communists are tried in London and gaoled for sedition: anti-Bolshevik feeling runs high.

1926

January: The year of the Charleston, a high-kicking dance craze from America. Women's skirts and hairstyles are at their shortest. John Logie Baird gives the first demonstration of a new invention called 'television' in his Soho workshop.

April: Princess Elizabeth born to the Duke and Duchess of York: she is third in line to the throne, after her father and uncle.

May: Britain's first and only General Strike brings the country to a standstill for ten days.

November: The Imperial Conference redefines the relationships between Britain and some of the Empire countries: some are rebranded as 'The British Commonwealth of Nations'.

1927

January: The British Broadcasting Company becomes the British Broadcasting Corporation with a unique charter guaranteeing its independence from the state.

September: London's first greyhound racing stadiums open at White City and Harringay.

November: London's first automatic telephone exchange opens at Holborn. The increasing strength of the Home Rule movement in India leads the British government to set up a commission of enquiry.

1928

January: The Thames bursts its banks in central London: the Tate Gallery and the Houses of Parliament suffer severe flood damage.

May: The Equal Franchise Act gives the vote to one and a half million women in Britain between the ages of twenty-one and thirty. London's electorate rises to 2.9 million.

September: Alexander Fleming, a professor at St Mary's Medical School, Paddington, accidentally discovers penicillin.

October: The Terror, the first British talking film, is premiered in London. Talkies take off the following year with *The Jazz Singer* starring Al Jolson.

1929

June: Britain acquires its second Labour government after the May election produces a stalemate. Turnout in London is 61%.

September: Britain and the USSR agree to restore diplomatic relations.

October: The Wall Street Crash sparks off an equivalent fall in share prices on the London Stock Exchange.

December: After several trials with yellow on the upper deck, red is confirmed as the colour of London buses.

Index